Insights You Need from
Harvard
Business
Review

STRATEGIC
ANALYTICS

Insights You Need from Harvard Business Review

Business is changing. Will you adapt or be left behind?

Get up to speed and deepen your understanding of the topics that are shaping your company's future with the **Insights You Need from Harvard Business Review** series. Featuring HBR's smartest thinking on fast-moving issues—blockchain, cybersecurity, AI, and more—each book provides the foundational introduction and practical case studies your organization needs to compete today and collects the best research, interviews, and analysis to get it ready for tomorrow.

You can't afford to ignore how these issues will transform the landscape of business and society. The Insights You Need series will help you grasp these critical ideas—and prepare you and your company for the future.

Books in the series include:

Agile

Artificial Intelligence

Blockchain

Climate Change

Customer Data and Privacy

Cybersecurity

Monopolies and Tech Giants

Strategic Analytics

The Year in Tech, 2021

Insights You Need from
**Harvard
Business
Review**

STRATEGIC
ANALYTICS

Harvard Business Review Press
Boston, Massachusetts

The web addresses referenced in this book were live and correct at the time of the book's publication but may be subject to change.

Library of Congress Cataloging-in-Publication Data

Title: Strategic analytics.
Other titles: Insights you need from Harvard Business Review.
Description: Boston, Massachusetts : Harvard Business Review Press, [2020] | Series: Insights you need from Harvard Business Review | Includes index.
Identifiers: LCCN 2019046714 (print) | LCCN 2019046715 (ebook) | ISBN 9781633698987 (paperback) | ISBN 9781633698994 (ebook)
Subjects: LCSH: Business planning. | Quantitative research. | Strategic planning—Computer programs. | Management—Statistical methods. | Management—Data processing.
Classification: LCC HD30.28 .S72916 2020 (print) | LCC HD30.28 (ebook) | DDC 658.4/012—dc23
LC record available at https://lccn.loc.gov/2019046714
LC ebook record available at https://lccn.loc.gov/2019046715

ISBN: 978-1-63369-898-7
eISBN: 978-1-63369-899-4

Contents

Contents

Section 2

Becoming an Analytics-Driven Organization

Section 3

Applying Data Analytics

Contents

Introduction

WHAT MAKES ANALYTICS STRATEGIC

by Thomas H. Davenport

Organizations are eager to reap the rewards of data and analytics—to learn about their customers by gathering vast amounts of data, to use that information to make better products and rise above the competition, and to enlist machine-learning algorithms to create new opportunities and improve performance. Yet, despite their efforts, many companies find that progress toward these goals is painfully slow. The successful use of analytics requires not only high-quality data and powerful hardware and software, but also a culture that encourages data-driven decisions and a set of skills to make them. Relatively few organizations have all those capabilities at scale.

Throughout most of the 60 or so years of business analytics, analytics have largely been tactical. They have described common and repetitive business transactions, they were largely backward-looking, and they weren't highly visible to (or desired by) senior executives. Smart managers certainly paid attention to the numbers showing how much money they made on specific products or in particular quarters, but that kind of routine reporting could hardly be described as strategic. Companies spent far more money and effort putting transactional information systems in place than they did on analyzing the data that emerged from them.

Decades later, we're using analytics in a much more dedicated manner. Around the turn of the century, companies started pursuing what might be called "strategic analytics"—analytics that were used to predict what customers might buy; to close less profitable stores, branches, and product lines; or even to develop new service offerings.[1] With the substantial performance improvements these efforts enabled, senior executives began to pay attention to the potential of analytics. In a few short years, analytics became the basis of their business strategy and their approach to the marketplace.[2] Capital One, for example, was spun out of a third-tier bank, but its credit card business was based on "information-based strategy." It employed data and analytics to make virtually every decision in the company—from what interest rate to charge to which customers to target. In doing so, Capital One returned more value to shareholders during its first 10 years as a public company than any other firm in the United States.

Analytics are reaching new heights with the addition of new technologies, much more data, machine learning, and artificial intelligence (AI). Companies are using external data to train algorithms to help with decision making. They're using internal data to improve employee performance. Leaders are hiring new talent—data scientists, statisticians, and analysts—to draw conclusions about their data and use these findings to inform leaders' strategic choices.

Strategic analytics are those that make a company's strategy or business model possible. Consider companies today whose business model would not be able to survive without analytics and AI, like Google—the employer of Cassie Kozyrkov, a contributor to this book—or the e-commerce operations of Vineyard Vines, described in chapter 10. These companies realize that by using analytics more strategically, they're seeing better results, faster.

Despite this realization, many organizations still struggle to implement analytics effectively. In a survey of nearly 65 *Fortune* 1000 or industry-leading firms, my colleague Randy Bean and I discovered that 72% of large, sophisticated companies have not achieved data-driven cultures.[3] Additionally, among those respondents:

- 69% reported that they have not created a data-driven organization

- 53% stated that they are not yet treating data as a business asset

- 52% admit that they are not competing on data and analytics

To truly leverage the value of strategic analytics, companies need to have some common elements in place.

Data and technology. Firms that succeed in strategic analytics either already possess large volumes of high-quality data and the technologies to manage them, or they do what is necessary to acquire them. That may involve sourcing external data, building digital infrastructures themselves, or turning to cloud computing.

The right talent and skill sets. Data-driven companies hire talented data scientists and quantitative analysts—often in large numbers. They build data teams around key talents and leverage those skills to reach their data goals.

And they ensure their people have basic data analysis skills, no matter their role in the organization, so they can understand what data is telling them and make decisions based on it.

A data-driven culture. Perhaps most importantly, firms that use analytics strategically have cultures that emphasize data- and analytics-driven decisions. This is perhaps the most difficult aspect of strategic analytics to achieve. Such a culture typically requires that senior executives set the tone for their organizations, sponsoring analytical projects and insisting on data-driven decisions when feasible.

This book aims to help anyone learn the basics of data and analytics, assist their companies in becoming more data-driven, and encourage the application of analytics to strategic issues and problems. It is divided into three parts. Section 1 introduces you to key concepts in the data space and helps you increase your data literacy, so you can be part of the conversation. Section 2 helps you learn how your organization can become data-driven—what needs to be in place and what to think about as you consider applying strategic analytics. Finally, section 3 helps you see the opportunities that data affords and gives you examples of ways to use your analytics for maximum benefit.

As you make your way through this book, consider whether you and your organization are prepared for strategic analytics by asking these questions:

- Do you personally have the skills you need either to analyze data or to consume it effectively?

- Do your people understand the basics of data and analytics? Do you have the right skills and talent on your team?

- Is your organization putting modern analytical technologies in place?

- Is this analytical horsepower being applied to problems and issues that will make the company more successful?

- Are the decisions your company makes using data to inform them? If not, are there ways to collect more information to make this shift?

- Does your organizational culture encourage analytical thinking from every member of your team?

If you're unsure about your answers to these questions—or you realize that your company isn't doing enough to make the most of its analytical capabilities—

it's time to engage with others in your company to address these issues and get started.

We may think of analytics as a field involving data and technology, but as many of the chapters in this book suggest, it is primarily about people. Their skills, priorities, and attitudes determine whether decisions and actions are taken on the basis of data and analysis, or intuition and guesswork. If your organization has enough people who care about strategic analytics—including yourself—the rest of the journey is relatively simple.

NOTES

1. Thomas H. Davenport, Jeanne G. Harris, David W. De Long, and Alvin L. Jacobson, "Data to Knowledge to Results: Building an Analytic Capability," *California Management Review* 43/2 (Winter 2001): 117–138.

2. Thomas H. Davenport, "Competing on Analytics," *Harvard Business Review*, January 2006, https://hbr.org/2006/01/competing-on-analytics; Thomas H. Davenport and Jeanne G. Harris, *Competing on Analytics: The New Science of Winning* (Boston: Harvard Business School Press, 2007).

3. Randy Bean and Thomas H. Davenport, "Companies are Failing in Their Efforts to Become Data-Driven," hbr.org, February 5, 2019, https://hbr.org/2019/02/companies-are-failing-in-their-efforts-to-become-data-driven.

Section 1

UNDERSTANDING ANALYTICS BASICS

THE FIVE ESSENTIAL ELEMENTS FOR SUCCEEDING WITH DATA

by Thomas C. Redman

There are plenty of great ideas and techniques in the data space: from analytics to machine learning to data-driven decision making to improving data quality. Some of these ideas have been around for a long time and are fully vetted, proving themselves again and again. Others have enjoyed wide socialization in the business, popular, and technical press. Indeed, the

Economist proclaimed that data is now "the world's most valuable asset."[1]

With all these success stories and such a heady reputation, one might expect to see companies trumpeting sustained revenue growth, permanent reductions in cost structures, dramatic improvements in customer satisfaction, and other benefits. Except for very few, this hasn't happened. Paradoxically, "data" appears everywhere but on the balance sheet and income statement. Indeed, the cold reality is that for most, progress is agonizingly slow.

It takes a lot to succeed with data. As figure 1-1 depicts, a company must perform solid work on five components, each reasonably aligned with the other four. Missing any of these elements compromises the total effort.

Let's explore each component in turn.

Quite obviously, to succeed in the data space, companies need *data*, properly defined, relevant to the tasks at hand, structured such that it is easy to find and understand, and of high-enough quality that it can be trusted. It helps if some of the data is proprietary, meaning that you have sole ownership of or access to it.

For most companies, data is a real problem. The data is scattered in silos—stuck in departmental systems that don't talk well with one another, the quality is poor, and the associated costs are high. Bad data makes it nearly impossible to become data-driven and adds enormous

FIGURE 1-1

Five essential elements for succeeding with data

And what happens when one element is missing.

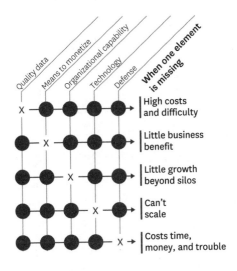

uncertainty to technological progress, including machine learning and digitization.

Then, companies need a *means to monetize that data,* essentially a business model for putting the data to work, at profit. This is where selling the data directly, building it into products and services, using it as input for analytics, and making better decisions come to the fore. There are so many ways to put data to work that it is hard to select the best ones. A high-level direction such as "using analytics wherever possible" is not enough. You have to define how you plan to use analytics to create business advantage and then execute. Without a clear, top-down business direction, people, teams, and entire departments go off on their own. There is lots of activity but little sustained benefit.

Organizational capabilities include talent, structure, and culture. Some years ago, I noted that most organizations were singularly "unfit for data." They lack the talent they need, they assign the wrong people to deal with quality, their organizational silos make data sharing difficult, and while they may claim that "data is our most important asset," they don't treat it that way. If anything, this problem has grown more acute.

Start with talent. It is obvious enough that if you want to push the frontiers of machine learning, you need a few world-class data scientists. Less obvious is the need for people who can rationalize business processes, build predictive models into them, and integrate the new technologies into the old. More generally, it is easy to bewail the shortage of top-flight technical talent, but just as important are skills up and down the organization chart, the management ability to pull it all together, and the leadership to drive execution at scale. Consider this example: Many companies see enormous potential in data-driven decision making. But to pursue such an objective, you have to teach people how to use data effectively. Leadership must realize that earning even a fraction of the value data offers takes more than simply bolting an AI program into one department or asking IT to digitize operations. Structure and culture are also a concern. As noted, organizational silos make it difficult to share data, effectively limiting the scope of the effort. All organizations claim that they value data, but their leaders are hard-pressed to answer basic questions such as, "Which data is most important?" "How do you plan to make money from your data?" or "Do you have anything that is proprietary?" Some even refer to data as "exhaust"—the antithesis of a valued asset! Without an abundance of talent and an organizational structure and culture that value data, it is difficult for companies to grow successful efforts beyond the team and department levels.

Fourth, companies need *technologies to deliver at scale and low cost*. Here, I include basic storage, processing, and communications technologies, as well as the more sophisticated architectures, analysis tools, and cognitive technologies that are the engines of monetization.

Quite obviously companies need technology—you simply can't scale and deliver without it. Facebook, Amazon, Netflix, and Google, who have succeeded with data, have built powerful platforms. Perhaps for these reasons, most companies begin their forays into the data space with technology. But from my vantage point, too many companies expect too much of technology, falling into the trap of viewing it as the primary driver of success. Technology is only one component.

The last element is *defense*, essentially minimizing risk. Defense includes actions such as following the law and regulations, keeping valued data safe from loss or theft, meeting privacy requirements, maintaining relationships with customers, matching the moves of a nimble competitor, staying in front of a better-funded behemoth, and steering clear of legal and regulatory actions that stem from monopoly power. You're unlikely to make much money from defense, but poor defense can cost you a lot of time, money, and trouble.

Thus, data requires a range of concerted effort. At a minimum, HR must find new talent and train everyone in the organization, tech departments must bring in new technologies and integrate them into existing infrastructures, privacy and security professionals must develop new policies and reach deep into the organization to enforce them, line organizations must deal with incredible disruption, everyone must contribute to data quality efforts, and leaders must set off in new, unfamiliar directions. Adding to complications, data, technology, and people are very different sorts of assets, requiring different management styles. It's a challenging transition.

Many companies have tried to resolve their data quality issues with the latest technology as a shortcut (for example, enterprise systems, data warehouses, cloud, blockchain), but these new systems have missed the mark.

It is important to remember that the goal is not simply to get all you can out of your data. Rather, you want to leverage your data in ways that create new growth, cut waste, increase customer satisfaction, or otherwise improve company performance. And "data" may present your best chance of achieving such goals. Successful data programs require concerted, sustained, properly informed, and coordinated effort.

TAKEAWAYS

Companies are investing time, energy, and resources on data strategies, but very few are seeing the sustained benefits of these efforts. To truly succeed, organizations must focus on five specific elements in the data space:

✓ **Quality data.** Companies need data that is properly defined, trustworthy, relevant to the tasks at hand, and structured in a way that makes it easy to find and understand.

✓ **Means to monetize that data.** Companies need a business model for putting that data to work profitably.

✓ **Organizational capabilities.** Companies need the right talent—both technical experts and general data skills up and down the org chart—as well as a structure and culture that allow data to be shared.

✓ **Technologies to deliver at scale and low cost.** Companies need basic technologies in place for data storage, processing, and communication, as well as more sophisticated technological tools, to help scale and deliver on their data efforts.

✓ **Defense.** Companies must minimize risk by following the law and regulations, focusing on cybersecurity and privacy, maintaining relationships with customers, and keeping an eye on competitors.

NOTE

1. "The World's Most Valuable Resource Is No Longer Oil, but Data," *Economist*, May 6, 2017, https://www.economist.com /leaders/2017/05/06/the-worlds-most-valuable-resource-is-no -longer-oil-but-data.

Adapted from "5 Ways Your Data Strategy Can Fail" on hbr.org, October 11, 2018 (product #H04KB5).

2

UNDERSTANDING THE TYPES OF DATA AND HOW THEY'RE CAPTURED

by Hugo Bowne-Anderson

T he ability to understand and communicate about data is an increasingly important skill for the 21st-century citizen, for three reasons. First, data science and AI are affecting many industries globally, from health care and government to agriculture and finance. Second, much of the news is reported through the lenses of data and predictive models. And third, so much of our personal data is being used to define how we interact with the world.

When so much data is informing decisions across so many industries, you need to have a basic understanding of the data ecosystem in order to be part of the discussion. On top of this, the industry that *you* work in will more likely than not see the impact of data analytics. Even if you yourself don't work directly with data, having this form of literacy will allow you to ask the right questions and be part of the conversation.

To take just one striking example, imagine if there had been a discussion around how to interpret probabilistic models in the run-up to the 2016 U.S. presidential election. FiveThirtyEight, the data journalism publication, gave Clinton a 71.4% chance of winning and Trump a 28.6% chance.[1] As Allen Downey, Professor of Computer Science at Olin College, points out, fewer people would have been shocked by the result had they been reminded that Trump winning, according to FiveThirtyEight's model, was a bit more likely than flipping two coins and getting two heads—hardly something that's impossible to conceive of.[2]

What We Talk About When We Talk About Data

The data-related concepts nontechnical people need to understand fall into five buckets: (i) data generation, collection, and storage, (ii) what data looks and feels like to data scientists and analysts, (iii) statistics intuition and common statistical pitfalls, (iv) model building, machine learning, and AI, and (v) the ethics of data, big and small.

The first four buckets roughly correspond to key steps in the data science hierarchy of needs, as proposed by data scientist and AI adviser Monica Rogati.[3] Although it has not yet been formally incorporated into data science workflows, I have added data ethics as the fifth key concept because ethics needs to be part of any conversation about data. So many people's lives, after all, are increasingly affected by the data they produce and the algorithms that use it. This article will focus on the first two concepts.

How Data Is Generated, Collected, and Stored

Every time you engage with the internet, whether via web browser or mobile app, your activity is detected and most often stored. To get a feel for some of what your basic web browser can detect, check out Clickclickclick .click, a project that opens a window into the extent of passive data collection online. If you are more adventurous, you can install the browser extension "data selfie," which "collect[s] the same information you provide to Facebook, while still respecting your privacy."[4]

The collection of data isn't relegated to merely the world of laptop, smartphone, and tablet interactions but the far wider internet of things, a catchall for traditionally dumb objects, such as radios and lights, that can be smartified by connecting them to the internet, along with any other data-collecting devices, such as fitness trackers, Amazon Echo, and self-driving cars.

All the collected data is stored in what we colloquially refer to as "the cloud," and it's important to clarify what's meant by this term. Firstly, data in cloud storage exists in physical space, just like on a computer or an external hard drive. The difference for the user is that the space it exists in is elsewhere, generally on server farms and data centers owned and operated by multinationals, and you usually access it over the internet. Cloud storage providers occur in two types, public and private. Public cloud services such as Amazon, Microsoft, and Google are responsible for data management and maintenance, whereas the responsibility for data in private clouds remains that of the company. Facebook, for example, has its own private cloud.

It is essential to recognize that cloud services store data in physical space, and the data may be subject to the laws of the country where the data is located. The General Data Protection Regulation (GDPR) in the EU impacts user data privacy and consent around personal data. Another pressing question is security, and we need to have a more public and comprehensible conversation around data security in the cloud.

The Feel of Data

Data scientists mostly encounter data in one of three forms: (i) tabular data (that is, data in a table, like a spreadsheet), (ii) image data, or (iii) unstructured data, such as natural language text or html code, which makes up the majority of the world's data.

Tabular data

The most common type for a data scientist to use is tabular data, which is analogous to a spreadsheet. In Robert Chang's article "Using Machine Learning to Predict Value of Homes on Airbnb," he shows a sample of the data, which appears in a table in which each row is a particular property and each column a particular feature of properties, such as host city, average nightly price, and one-year revenue. (Note that data is rarely delivered directly from the user to tabular data; data engineering is an essential step to make data ready for such an analysis.)

Such data is used to train, or teach, machine-learning models to predict Lifetime Values (LTV) of properties, that is, how much revenue they will bring in over the course of the relationship.

Image data

Image data is data that consists of, well, images. Many of the successes of deep learning have occurred in the realm of image classification. The ability to diagnose disease from imaging data, such as diagnosing cancerous tissue from combined PET and CT scans, and the ability of self-driving cars to detect and classify objects in their field of vision are two of many use cases of image data. To work with image data, a data scientist will convert an image into a grid (or matrix) of red-green-blue pixel values or numbers and use these matrices as inputs to their predictive models.

Unstructured data

Unstructured data is, as one might guess, data that isn't organized in either of the previous manners. Part of the data scientist's job is to structure such data so it may be analyzed. Natural language, or text, provides the clearest example. One common method of turning textual data into structured data is to represent it as word counts, so that "the cat chased the mouse" becomes "(cat,1),(chased,1), (mouse,1),(the,2)". This is called a bag-of-words model and allows us to compare texts, to compute distances between them, and to combine them into clusters. Bag-of-words performs surprisingly well for many practical applications, especially considering that it doesn't distinguish "build bridges not walls" from "build walls not bridges." Part of the game here is to turn textual data into numbers that we can feed into predictive models, and the principle is very similar between bag-of-words and more sophisticated methods. Such methods allow for sentiment analysis ("is a text positive, negative, or neutral?") and text classification ("is a given article news, entertainment, or sport?"), among many others. For an example of text classification, check out Cloudera Fast Forward Labs' prototype Newsie.

These are just two of the five steps to working with data, but they're essential starting points for data literacy. When you're dealing with data, think about how the data was collected and what kind of data it is. That will help you understand its meaning, how much to trust it, and how much work needs to be done to convert it into a useful form.

TAKEAWAYS

The ability to understand and communicate about data is an increasingly important skill. Even if you don't work directly with data, data literacy will allow you to ask the right questions and be part of the conversation.

✓ There are five data-related concepts nontechnical people need to understand:

 1. data generation, collection, and storage

 2. what data looks and feels like to data scientists and analysts

 3. statistics intuition and common statistical pitfalls

 4. model building, machine learning, and AI

 5. the ethics of data

✓ Data is usually in one of three forms: tabular data, image data, or unstructured data. Tabular data appears on tables or spreadsheets. Image data can be converted into values and used as inputs to predictive models. Unstructured data, such as natural language text or html code, isn't organized and makes up most of the world's data.

NOTES

1. Nate Silver, "Final Election Update: There's a Wide Range of Outcomes, and Most of Them Come Up Clinton," FiveThirtyEight, November 8, 2016, https://fivethirtyeight.com/features/final -election-update-theres-a-wide-range-of-outcomes-and-most-of -them-come-up-clinton/.

2. Allen Downey, "Why Are We So Surprised?" *Probably Overthinking It* (blog), November 14, 2016, http://allendowney.blogspot .com/2016/11/why-are-we-so-surprised.html.

3. Monica Rogati, "The AI Hierarchy of Needs," Hackernoon, June 12, 2017, https://hackernoon.com/the-ai-hierarchy-of-needs -18f111fcc007.

4. Jen Caltrider, "Prepare to Be Creeped Out," *The Mozilla Blog*, March 15, 2018, https://blog.mozilla.org/blog/2018/03/15/prepare -to-be-creeped-out/.

Adapted from "Your Data Literacy Depends on Understanding the Types of Data and How They're Captured" on hbr.org, October 23, 2018 (product #H04M6H).

3

THE RIGHT WAY TO DEPLOY PREDICTIVE ANALYTICS

by Eric Siegel

With today's high demand for data scientists and the high salaries that they command, it's often not practical for companies to keep them on staff. Instead, many organizations work to ramp up their existing staff's analytics skills, including predictive analytics. But organizations need to proceed with caution. Predictive analytics is especially easy to get wrong. Here are the first three "don'ts" your team needs to learn and their corresponding remedies.

1. Don't Fall for Buzzwords—Clarify Your Objective

You know the Joe Jackson song, "You Can't Get What You Want (Till You Know What You Want)"? Turn it on and let it be your mantra. As fashionable as it is, "data science" is not a business objective or a learning objective in and of itself. This buzzword means nothing more specific than "some clever use of data." It doesn't necessarily refer to any particular technology, method, or value proposition. Rather, it alludes to a culture—one of smart people doing creative things to find value in their data. It's important for everyone to keep this top of mind when learning to work with data.

Under the wide umbrella of data science sits predictive analytics, which delivers the most actionable win you can get from data. In a nutshell, predictive analytics is technology that learns from experience (data) to predict the future behavior of individuals in order to drive better decisions. Prediction is the Holy Grail for more effectively executing mass-scale operations in marketing, financial risk, fraud detection, and more. Predictive analytics empowers your organization to optimize these functions by flagging who's most likely to click, buy, lie, die, commit fraud, quit their job, or cancel their subscription—and, beyond predicting people, by also foretelling the most likely outcomes for individual corporate clients and financial instruments. These predictions directly inform the action to take with each individual, for example, by marketing to those most likely to buy and auditing those most likely to commit fraud.

In their application to these business functions, *predictive analytics* and *machine learning (ML)* are synonyms (in other arenas, machine learning also extends to tasks such as facial recognition that aren't usually called predictive analytics). Machine learning is key to prediction. The accumulation of patterns or formulas ML derives (learns) from the data—known as a *predictive model*—serves to consider a unique situation and put odds on the outcome. For example, the model could take as input everything currently known about an individual customer and produce as output the probability that that individual will cancel their subscription.

When you begin to deploy predictive analytics with your team, you're embarking on a new kind of value proposition, so it requires a new kind of leadership process. You'll need some team members to become "machine-learning leaders" or "predictive-analytics managers," titles that signify much more specific skill sets than the catchall "data scientist," which can be vague and overhyped (but do allow them that title if they like, as long as you're on the same page).

2. Don't Lead with Software Selection— Team Skills Come First

In 2011, Thomas Davenport was kind enough to deliver the keynote address at the conference I founded, Predictive Analytics World. "It's not about the math—it's about the people!" he absolutely bellowed at our captivated audience, more loudly than I'd ever heard since high school, when teachers had to get control of a classroom of teens.

Tom's startling tone struck just the right note (a high D flat, to be exact). Analytics vendors will tell you their software is The Solution. But the solution to what? The problem at hand is to optimize your large-scale operations. And the solution is a new way of business that integrates machine learning. So, a machine-learning tool only serves a small part of what must be a holistic organizational process.

Rather than following a vendor's lead, prepare your staff to manage machine-learning integration as an enterprise endeavor, and then allow them to determine a more informed choice of analytics software during a later stage of the project.

3. Don't Leap to the Number Crunching— Strategically Plan the Deployment

The most common mistake that derails predictive analytics projects is jumping into machine learning before establishing a path to operational deployment. Predictive analytics isn't a technology you simply buy and plug in. It's an organizational paradigm that must bridge the quant/business culture gap by way of a collaborative process guided jointly by strategic, operational, and analytical stakeholders.

Each predictive analytics project follows a relatively standard, established series of steps that begins with establishing how it will be deployed by your business and then works backward to see what you need to predict and what data you need to predict it, as follows:

1. Establish the business objective. Decide how the predictive model will be integrated in order to actively make a positive impact on existing operations, such as by more effectively targeting customer retention marketing campaigns.

2. Define a specific prediction objective to serve the business objective. For this, you must have buy-in from

business stakeholders, such as marketing staff, who are willing to change their targeting accordingly. Here's an example: *"Which current customers with a tenure of at least one year and who have purchased more than $500 to date will cancel within three months and not rejoin for another three months thereafter?"* In practice, business tactics and pragmatic constraints will often mean the prediction objective must be even more specifically defined than that.

3. **Prepare the training data that machine learning will operate on.** This can be a significant bottleneck, generally expected to require 80% of the project's hands-on workload. It's a database-programming task, by which your existing data in its current form is rejiggered for the needs of machine-learning software.

4. **Apply machine learning to generate the predictive model.** This is the "rocket science" part, but it isn't the most time intensive. It's the stage where the choice of analytics tool counts—but, initially, you can try and compare software options with free evaluation licenses before making a decision about which one to buy (or which free open-source tool to use).

5. **Deploy the model.** Integrate its predictions into existing operations. For example, target a retention campaign to the top 5% of customers for whom an affirmative answer to the "will the customer cancel" question defined in step 2 is most probable.

There are two things you should know about these steps before selecting training options for your predictive analytics leaders. First, these five steps involve extensive backtracking and iteration. For example, only by executing step 3 might it become clear there isn't sufficient data for the prediction objective established in step 2, in which case the earlier step must be revisited and modified.

Second, at least for your first pilot projects, you'll need to bring in an external machine-learning consultant for key parts of the process. Normally, your staff shouldn't endeavor to immediately become autonomous hands-on practitioners of the core machine learning, that is, step 4. While it's important for project leaders to learn the fundamental principles behind how the technology works—in order to understand both its data requirements and the meaning of the predictive probabilities it outputs—a quantitative expert with prior predictive analytics projects in his or her portfolio should step in for step 4, and also help guide steps 2 and 3. This can be a relatively light engagement that keeps the overall project cost-effective, since you'll still internally execute the most time-intensive steps.

Good luck, and happy predicting.

Many organizations work to ramp up their existing staff's analytics skills, including in predictive analytics, instead of hiring expensive data science talent. To do so effectively, organizations should:

✓ Clarify objectives for what the team needs to learn. Focus on a specific skill set or role, such as becoming a "predictive analytics manager," rather than something like "data scientist," which can be vague.

✓ Emphasize skills before looking at software selection. A machine-learning tool only serves a small part of what must be a larger organizational process. Prepare teams to manage machine-learning integration first, and hold off selecting analytics software until later.

✓ Avoid jumping to number crunching. Each predictive analytics project follows a series of steps that begins first by establishing how it will be deployed and then working backward to see what you need to predict and what data you need to predict it.

✓ Pilot projects will likely require an external machine-learning consultant for key parts of the process. A quantitative expert should step in to help define the prediction objective, prepare the training data, and apply machine learning to generate the model.

Adapted from "3 Common Mistakes That Can Derail Your Team's Predictive Analytics Efforts" on hbr.org, October 5, 2018 (product #H04KHM).

WHAT GREAT DATA ANALYSTS DO

by Cassie Kozyrkov

T he top trophy hire in data science is elusive, and that should be no surprise: A "full-stack" data scientist has mastery of machine learning, statistics, and analytics. When teams can't get their hands on a three-in-one polymath, they set their sights on luring the most impressive prize among the single-origin specialists. Which of those skills gets the podium?

Today's fashion in data science favors flashy sophistication with a dash of sci-fi, making AI and machine learning the darlings of the job market. Alternative challengers for the alpha spot come from statistics, thanks to a century-long reputation for rigor and mathematical superiority. What about analytics?

Analytics as a Second-Class Citizen

If your primary skill is analytics (or data mining or business intelligence), chances are that your self-confidence has taken a beating as machine learning and statistics have become prized within companies, the job market, and the media.

But what the uninitiated rarely grasp is that although these three professions may all fall under data science, they are completely different from one another. They may use some of the same methods and equations, but that's where the similarity ends. Far from being a lesser version of the other data science breeds, good analysts are a prerequisite for effectiveness in your data endeavors. It's dangerous to have them quit on you, but that's exactly what they'll do if you underappreciate them.

Instead of asking analysts to develop their statistics or machine-learning skills, consider encouraging them to seek the heights of their own discipline first. In data science, excellence in one area beats mediocrity in two. So, let's examine what it means to be truly excellent in each of the data science disciplines, what value these different experts bring, and which personality traits are required to survive each job. Doing so will help explain why analysts are valuable, and how organizations should use them.

Excellence in Statistics: Rigor

Statisticians are specialists in coming to conclusions beyond your data safely—they are your best protection against fooling yourself in an uncertain world. To them, inferring something sloppily is a greater sin than leaving your mind a blank slate, so expect a good statistician to put the brakes on your exuberance. They care deeply about whether the methods applied are right for the problem and they agonize over which inferences are valid from the information at hand.

The result? A perspective that helps leaders make important decisions in a risk-controlled manner. In other words, they use data to minimize the chance that you'll come to an unwise conclusion.

Excellence in Machine Learning: Performance

You might be an applied machine-learning/AI engineer if your response to "I bet you couldn't build a model that passes testing at 99.99999% accuracy" is "Watch me." With the coding chops to build both prototypes and production systems that work and the stubborn resilience to fail every hour for several years if that's what it takes, machine-learning specialists know that they won't find the perfect solution in a textbook. Instead, they'll be engaged in a marathon of trial and error. Having great intuition for how long it'll take them to try each new option is a huge plus and is more valuable than an intimate knowledge of how the algorithms work (though it's nice to have both). Performance means more than clearing a metric—it also means reliable, scalable, and easy-to-maintain models that perform well in production. Engineering excellence is a must.

The result? A system that automates a tricky task well enough to pass your statistician's strict testing bar and deliver the audacious performance a business leader demands.

Wide Versus Deep

What the previous two roles have in common is that they both provide high-effort solutions to specific problems. If the problems they tackle aren't worth solving, you end up wasting their time and your money. A frequent lament among business leaders is, "Our data science group is useless." And the problem usually lies in an absence of analytics expertise.

Statisticians and machine-learning engineers are narrow-and-deep workers—the shape of a rabbit hole, incidentally—so it's really important to point them at problems that deserve the effort. If your experts are carefully solving the wrong problems, your investment in data science will suffer low returns. To ensure that you can make good use of narrow-and-deep experts, you either need to be sure you already have the right problem or you need a wide-and-shallow approach to finding one.

Excellence in Analytics: Speed

The best analysts are lightning-fast coders who can surf vast data sets quickly, encountering and surfacing potential insights faster than those other specialists can say "whiteboard." Their semi-sloppy coding style baffles traditional software engineers—but leaves them in the dust. Speed is their highest virtue, closely followed by the ability to identify potentially useful gems. A mastery of visual presentation of information helps, too: beautiful and effective plots allow the mind to extract information faster, which pays off in time-to-potential-insights.

The result is that the business gets a finger on its pulse and eyes on previously unknown unknowns. This generates the inspiration that helps decision makers select valuable quests to send statisticians and ML engineers on, saving them from mathematically impressive excavations of useless rabbit holes.

Sloppy Nonsense or Stellar Storytelling?

"But," object the statisticians, "most of their so-called insights are nonsense." By that they mean the results of their exploration may reflect only noise. Perhaps, but there's more to the story.

Analysts are data storytellers. Their mandate is to summarize interesting facts and to use data for inspiration. In some organizations those facts and that inspiration become input for human decision makers. But in more sophisticated data operations, data-driven inspiration gets flagged for proper statistical follow-up.

Good analysts have unwavering respect for the one golden rule of their profession: Do not come to conclusions beyond the data (and prevent your audience from doing it, too). To this end, one way to spot a good analyst is that they use softened, hedging language. For example, not "we conclude" but "we are inspired to wonder." They also discourage leaders' overconfidence by emphasizing a multitude of possible interpretations for every insight.

As long as analysts stick to the facts—saying only "This is what is here"—and don't take themselves too seriously, the worst crime they could commit is wasting someone's time when they run their findings by them.

While statistical skills are required to test hypotheses, analysts are your best bet for coming up with those hypotheses in the first place. For instance, an analyst might say something like "It's only a correlation, but I suspect it could be driven by . . ." and then explain why they think that. This takes strong intuition about what might be going on beyond the data and the communication skills to convey the options to the decision maker, who typically calls the shots on which hypotheses (of many) are important enough to warrant a statistician's effort. As analysts mature, they'll begin to get the hang of judging what's important in addition to what's interesting, allowing decision makers to step away from the middleman role.

Of the three breeds, analysts are the most likely heirs to the decision throne. Because subject-matter expertise goes a long way toward helping you spot interesting patterns in your data faster, the best analysts are serious about familiarizing themselves with the domain. Failure to do so is a red flag. As their curiosity pushes them to develop a sense for the business, expect their output to shift from a jumble of false alarms to a sensibly curated set of insights that decision makers are more likely to care about.

Analytics for Decision Making

To avoid wasting time, analysts should lay out the story they're tempted to tell and poke it from several angles with follow-up investigations to see if it holds water before bringing it to decision makers. The decision maker should then function as a filter between exploratory data analytics and statistical rigor. If someone with decision responsibility finds the analyst's exploration promising for a decision they have to make, they then can sign off on a statistician spending the time to do a more rigorous analysis. (This process indicates why just telling analysts to get better at statistics misses the point in an important way. Not only are the two activities separate, but another person sits in between them, meaning it's not necessarily any more efficient for one person to do both things.)

Analytics for Machine Learning and AI

Machine-learning specialists put a bunch of potential data inputs through algorithms, tweak the settings, and keep iterating until the right outputs are produced. While it may sound like there's no role for analytics here, in practice a business often has far too many potential ingredients to shove into the blender all at once. One way to filter down to a promising set of inputs to try is domain expertise—ask a human with opinions about how things might work. Another way is through analytics. To use the analogy of cooking, the machine-learning engineer is great at tinkering in the kitchen, but right now they're standing in front of a huge, dark warehouse full of potential ingredients. They could either start grabbing them haphazardly and dragging them back to their kitchens, or they could send a sprinter armed with a flashlight through the warehouse first. Your analyst is the sprinter; their ability to quickly help you see and summarize what is there is a superpower for your process.

The Dangers of Underappreciating Analysts

An excellent analyst is not a shoddy version of the machine-learning engineer; their coding style is optimized for speed—on purpose. Nor are they a bad statistician, since they don't deal at all with uncertainty; they deal with facts. The primary job of the analyst is to say: "Here's what's in our data. It's not my job to talk about what it means, but perhaps it will inspire the decision maker to pursue the question with a statistician."

If you overemphasize hiring and rewarding skills in machine learning and statistics, you'll lose your analysts. Who will help you figure out which problems are worth solving then? You'll be left with a group of miserable experts who keep being asked to work on useless projects or analytics tasks they didn't sign up for. Your data will lie around useless.

When in doubt, hire analysts before other roles. Appreciate them and reward them. Encourage them to grow to the heights of their chosen career (and not someone else's). Of the cast of characters mentioned in this story, the only ones that every business needs are decision makers and analysts. The others you'll only be able to use when you know exactly what you need them for. Start with analytics, and be proud of your newfound ability to open your eyes to the rich and beautiful information in front of you. Data-driven inspiration is a powerful thing.

TAKEAWAYS

Companies want data scientists who specialize in machine learning, statistics, and analytics. But when this expertise isn't available, hiring managers should look for analysts. Data analysts provide distinct advantages to organizations.

✓ Statisticians offer rigor and machine-learning specialists provide performance. But analysts work fast—their coding style is optimized for speed—and are masters of data visualization.

✓ Analysts are storytellers, summarizing interesting facts and using data as inspiration. They question the data, asking what the information could be indicating, rather than presenting conclusions. They're the best bet for coming up with problems to solve and hypotheses to test.

✓ Analysts look at information from several angles and dig into it deeply before bringing it to decision makers. The decision maker then makes the call as to whether more rigorous analysis is necessary, usually by a statistician.

Adapted from "What Great Data Analysts Do—and Why Every Organization Needs Them" on hbr.org, December 4, 2018 (product #H04OLF).

5

WHAT DATA IS AND ISN'T GOOD FOR

by Joel Shapiro

L eaders today increasingly turn to big data and advanced analytics in hopes of solving their most pressing problems, whether it's a drop-off of repeat customers, a shift in consumption patterns, or an attempt to reach new markets. The prevailing thought is that more data is better, especially given advancements in tools and technologies such as artificial intelligence and predictive analytics.

But when it comes to uncovering the motivations and rationale behind individual behaviors within a social system, data can only do so much. It can guide the discovery of a problem, but it won't determine the solution. In other words, data analytics can tell you *what* is happening, but it will rarely tell you *why*. To effectively bring together the what and the why—a problem and its cause, in order to find a probable solution—leaders need to combine the advanced capabilities of big data and analytics with tried-and-true qualitative approaches such as interviewing groups of individuals, conducting focus groups, and in-depth observation.

In my conversations with business leaders about how they use data analytics, a primary focus is on technical, large-scale systems. This is where big data and analytics can really shine, in applications such as predictive maintenance. Industrial companies, from railroads to oil fields, use predictive analytics to ensure smooth operations; rather than wait for a mechanical breakdown to occur, predictive maintenance prevents problems and avoids downtime.

What works with locomotives and oil rigs, however, can be far less effective when it comes to influencing people's behaviors. With social systems and the behaviors generated by large groups of individuals—who does what and under what conditions—it is far harder to identify solutions to problems. This points to the shortcoming of using data analytics alone for solving problems that arise from individual behavior.

That's not to say big data and analytics don't play an important part. Rather, by understanding the strengths and limitations of using big data in this way, leaders can employ the most effective strategies for identifying the what and why of a problem, and how to solve it—and can help their teams learn to do the same. Here are five important considerations that everyone who works with big data needs to understand:

1. **Data can determine the "what" of a problem.** Data analysis is helpful in determining patterns of behavior, both positive and negative—for example, the success of an organization or enterprise in motivating people to engage in certain activities. Analyses may reveal, for instance, that a certain type of customer is more or less likely to buy a particular product or renew a subscription or membership. Sophisticated data analytics can reveal patterns among large groups and smaller subgroups.

2. **Data rarely reveals the "why."** In the aggregate, individual behaviors show up in the data, revealing patterns among certain demographics and groups. But just because data shows, say, what the typical 33-year-old woman making less than $100,000 a year who has children is likely to do or not do, that won't reveal the *why*. Data may prompt people to

make assumptions; for instance, that a price point was too high for a particular customer, or that a subscription service related to a leisure activity (for example, a gym membership) no longer appeals to a consumer who has time constraints. Assumptions also can be made about root causes of behaviors, such as why millennials prefer companies that prioritize social impact or why a particular subgroup of employees underperforms. Assumptions, though, are only guesses about the rationale of others' behaviors, not a reliable basis for determining the best solution to address a problem.

3. **The "why" needs a qualitative approach.** Whether the social group involves current customers, potential customers, vendors, or any other population, the only way to discover the "why" is to engage with them in qualitative research such as interviews, focus groups, and observation. The result is an iterative process that starts with the "who" and the "what," which the data can reveal, and proceeds to the next step of diagnosing the "why," which the data cannot typically reveal. In the past, companies often hired experts in qualitative research to help determine how and why customers use par-

ticular products or gravitated to certain brands. Today, though, many business leaders try to use big data and analytics to automate the entire process. But the shortcomings of using data for diagnostics of social behaviors are quickly revealed. For example, social media analytics can identify influencers for well-defined customer segments. But the real challenge is knowing *why* customers are drawn to those influencers in order to craft effective strategies to entice customers to buy more or become brand advocates themselves.

4. **You need to consider temporal and other factors.** Other factors also influence behavior, making solutions more difficult to find and less likely to remain effective over time. For example, several years ago, an auto club discovered that motorists who had longer-than-average wait times by the side of the road were less likely to renew their subscriptions. Based on that data, the company emphasized the need to reduce wait times. Since then, the proliferation of smartphones and other devices has given people ways to occupy themselves, altering their perception of how long they're waiting. As a result, focusing on wait time alone today

(as opposed to other factors such as pricing and quality) has proved to be less effective in reducing churn among auto club members.

5. **You need rigorous testing to find the right solution.** With big data analysis and smaller-scale qualitative research combined, organizations can gain deeper insights into both problems and their causes, which can then help inform solutions that are likely to produce a desired result. The best way to know the effectiveness of a solution is to conduct randomized testing using two similar groups: one that is offered the solution and one that is not. Data analysis from this experimentation will reveal whether the solution actually solves the problem. Although randomized experiments can be expensive and complex, the data analysis involved brings the process full circle and often pays for itself in terms of the return on investment.

Data analytics are most effective as part of an overall process to identify, explore, and test, but they are not the only tool for the task. Solving social behaviors still requires small-scale qualitative exploration to engage people and learn more about what's truly motivating the behaviors that show up in the data.

TAKEAWAYS

Data can only do so much. It can tell you *what* is happening, but it will rarely tell you *why*. To bring the two together, leaders need to combine the advanced capabilities of big data and analytics with qualitative approaches.

✓ Individual patterns can show up in data, revealing the "what" of a problem. Upon seeing these patterns, people may make assumptions about the root causes of the behavior. But these assumptions are only guesses and are not reliable for determining a solution.

✓ To discover the "why," engage in qualitative research, such as conducting interviews and focus groups and using in-depth observation. Also consider what other factors that can't be seen in the numbers may be affecting the data.

✓ Finally, you must perform randomized testing. This experimentation will allow you to see whether your proposed solution might solve the problem.

Adapted from "Help Your Team Understand What Data Is and Isn't Good For" on hbr.org, October 12, 2018 (product #H04L9Y).

Section 2

BECOMING AN ANALYTICS-DRIVEN ORGANIZATION

6

PRIORITIZE WHICH DATA SKILLS YOUR COMPANY NEEDS

by Chris Littlewood

Data skills—the skills to turn data into insight and action—are the driver of modern economies. According to the World Economic Forum, computing and mathematically focused jobs are showing the strongest growth, at the expense of less quantitative roles (see figure 6-1).[1]

So whether it's to maximize the part we play in data-driven economic growth, or simply to ensure that we and

FIGURE 6-1

Jobs built on data skills are showing the strongest growth

Average compound employment annual growth rate %, 2015–2020

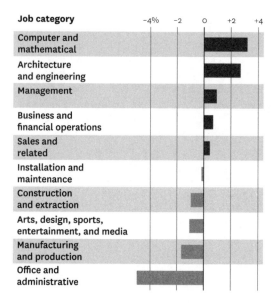

Source: World Economic Forum's "The Future of Jobs" survey, 2016

our teams remain relevant and employable, we need to think about transitioning to a more data-skewed skill set. But which skills should we focus on? Can most of us expect to keep pace with this trend ourselves, or would we be better off retreating to shrinking areas of the economy, leaving data skills to the specialists?

To help answer this question, we rebooted and adapted an approach we took to prioritizing Microsoft Excel skills according to the benefits and costs of acquiring them. We applied a time-utility analysis to the field of data skills. "Time" is time to learn—a proxy for the opportunity cost to you or your team of acquiring the skill. "Utility" is how much you're likely to need the skill, a proxy for the value it adds to the corporation, and your own career prospects.

Combine time and utility, and you get a simple two-by-two matrix with four quadrants, as depicted in figure 6-2:

- **Learn:** high utility, low time-to-learn. This is low-hanging fruit that will add value for you and your team quickly.

- **Plan:** high utility, high time-to-learn. While this is valuable, acquiring this skill will mean prioritizing it ahead of other learning and activities. You need to be sure that it's worth the investment.

- **Browse:** low utility, low time-to-learn. You don't need this now, but it's easy to acquire so stay aware in case its utility increases.

- **Ignore:** low utility, high time-to-learn. You don't have the time for this.

FIGURE 6-2

Which data skills should you learn first?

Make the most of your limited learning time.

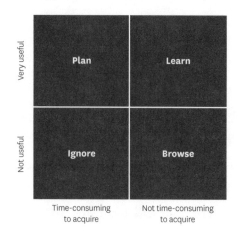

Source: Filtered

In order to help you decide where to focus your development effort, we have plotted key data skills against this framework. We long-listed skills associated with roles such as business analyst, data analyst, data scientist, machine-learning engineer, or growth hacker. We then prioritized them for impact based on how frequently they appear in job postings, press reports, and our own learner feedback. And finally, we coupled this with information on how difficult the skills are to learn—using time to competence as a metric and assessing the depth and breadth of each skill.

We did this for techniques, rather than for specific technologies: so, for machine learning rather than TensorFlow, for business intelligence rather than Microsoft Excel, etc. Once you've worked out which techniques are priorities in your context, you can then work out which specific software and associated skills best support them.

You can also apply this framework to your own context, where the impact of data skills might be different. Figure 6-3 shows our results.

At Filtered, we found that constructing this matrix helped us to make hard decisions about where to focus: At first sight, all the skills in our long list seemed valuable. But realistically, we can only hope to move the needle on a few, at least in the short term. We concluded that the best return on investment in skills for our company was in data visualization, based on its high utility and low time to learn. We've already acted on our analysis and have just started to use Tableau to improve the way we present usage analysis to clients.

Try the matrix in your own company to help your team determine which data skills are most important for them to start learning now.

FIGURE 6-3

An example of how to plot data skills on a 2×2 learning matrix

How one company plotted its own internal learning needs.

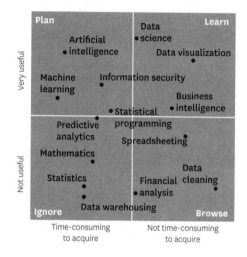

Source: Analysis of internal data learning needs by Filtered

TAKEAWAYS

When it comes to growing data capabilities within your company, you can't learn everything at once. Every organization has unique needs, and thinking about the time each skill takes to learn and its usefulness will help you decide which areas to focus on first. You can plot these on a two-by-two matrix and sort them into four groups:

✓ **Learn:** These skills have high utility and low time-to-learn. Skills in this quadrant will add value for you and your team quickly.

✓ **Plan:** These skills also have high utility but require time to learn. Acquiring these skills will mean prioritizing them over others, so you need to make sure they're worth the investment.

✓ **Browse:** Skills in this quadrant have low utility and low time-to-learn. You likely don't need these immediately, but they're easy to acquire later, if necessary.

✓ **Ignore:** These skills have low utility and take time to learn. You don't have time for these and can skip them.

NOTE

1. World Economic Forum, "Employment Trends" in *The Future of Jobs Report*, http://reports.weforum.org/future-of-jobs-2016/employment-trends/.

Adapted from "Prioritize Which Data Skills Your Company Needs with This 2×2 Matrix" on hbr.org, October 18, 2018 (product #H04KOL).

HOW A GERMAN MANUFACTURING COMPANY SET UP ITS ANALYTICS LAB

by Niklas Goby, Tobias Brandt, and Dirk Neumann

O ver the past few years, most businesses have come to recognize that the ability to collect and analyze the data they generate has become a key source of competitive advantage.

ZF, a global automotive supplier based in Germany, was no exception. Digital startups had begun producing virtual products that ZF did not know how to compete against, and engineers in logistics, operations, and other functions were finding that their traditional approaches couldn't handle the complex issues they faced. Some company executives had begun to fear they were in for their own "Kodak moment"—a fatal disruption that could redefine their business and eliminate overnight advantages accumulated over decades. With automotive analysts forecasting major changes in mobility, they began to think that the firm needed a dedicated lab that focused entirely on data challenges.

But how?

At the time one of us, Niklas, a data scientist for ZF, was pursuing a PhD part-time at the University of Freiburg. Niklas took the first step and recruited his advisers at the university, Dirk Neumann and Tobias Brandt, to help him set up a lab for the company. This gave ZF access to top-notch expertise in data analytics and the management of information systems.

The hardest part was figuring out how the lab would work. After all, industrial data laboratories are a fairly new phenomenon—we couldn't just download a blueprint. However, after a number of stumbles, we succeeded in winning acceptance for the lab and figured out a number of best practices that we think are broadly applicable to almost any data lab.

1. Focus on the Right Internal Customers

ZF had dozens of departments filled with potentially high-impact data-related projects. Although we were tempted to tackle many projects across the entire company, we realized that to create visibility within a 146,000-employee firm, we had to focus on the most promising departments and projects first.

But how would we define "most promising"? As the goal of the data lab is to create value by analyzing data, we initially focused on the departments that generate the most data. Unfortunately, this didn't narrow it down a whole lot. The finance, logistics, marketing, and sales departments—as well as production and quality—all produced large amounts of data that could be interesting for data-science pilot projects.

However, we knew from experience that the lowest-hanging fruits for high-impact projects in a manufacturing company like ZF would be in production and quality. For years, ZF's production lines had been connected and controlled by MES and ERP systems, but the data they generated had yet to be deeply tapped. We decided, therefore, to begin by concentrating on production issues, such as interruptions, rework rates, and throughput speed, where we could have an immediate impact.

2. Identifying High-Impact Problems

Next, we selected those projects within production and quality that promised the highest-value outcomes. Our experience with the first few projects provided the basis for a project evaluation model, which we have continued to refine. The model contained a set of criteria along three dimensions that helped us to rank projects.

- **The problem to be solved had to be clearly defined.** We could not adopt an abstract aim such as "improve production." We needed a clear idea of how the analysis would create business value.

- **Hard data had to play a major role in the solution.** And the data had to be available, accessible, and of good quality. We needed to shield the team from being flooded by business intelligence reporting projects.

- **The team had to be motivated.** We gave project teams independence in choosing how they solved the problems they took on. And while we made the budget tight enough to enforce focus, we made sure that it was not so tight that the team couldn't make basic allocation decisions on its own. To sustain motivation and enthusiasm, we prioritized projects that could be subdivided into smaller but more easily achieved goals.

While we eventually found it useful to assign a specific individual to manage relations with the rest of the company, we kept the whole lab involved in project selection as the number of people working in the lab grew. This kept everyone informed, gave them a greater sense of personal responsibility, and implicitly expressed management's appreciation for their professional judgment.

3. Execution

The key risk was that the team would get lost in optimizing minor nuances of models and methods instead of solving the major problem. To avoid this, we usually limited the execution phase to three months, and gave the team the right to cancel its engagement.

This power turned out to be a game changer. Giving the team (including the domain expert) a "nuclear option" made them much more focused and goal-oriented. Once we put this rule in place, the number of change requests from the internal client dropped, and the information initially provided tended to be more accurate and complete than before.

Of course, a team couldn't cancel a project for arbitrary reasons. It needed to justify its decision, specifying conditions under which the project could be reopened. And while cancellations are contentious, they are sometimes necessary to free resources and to enforce progress toward a meaningful goal. In fact, introducing the ability to cancel projects actually increased the number of successfully completed projects.

Although a single team can work on multiple projects concurrently, particularly as waiting for responses from the client department can lead to delays, we generally found it best for the team to work on a single project at a time. We found that downtimes were better used by team members to learn new analytics methods and techniques, which continued to advance at a rapid pace.

We kept our internal customer up to date on our progress through regular reports and when possible by including its domain expert in the project team. If we could not do so, we looked for an arrangement—such as a weekly meeting—that allowed us to contact the domain expert directly without having to pass through gatekeepers.

Key Success Factors

Beyond gaining a general understanding of the data lab's work as a three-stage process, we learned other lessons too. Specifically, we found three more ingredients to be crucial to the data lab's success:

- **Executive support.** The confidence that the technology executive team placed in us was crucial to our success. Fortunately, the team didn't seem to regret it: "Giving the data lab great freedom to act independently, to try ideas, and also to accept failures as part of a learning process, required trust. But the momentum it created is something we do not want to miss," said Dr. Jürgen Sturm, Chief Information Officer.

- **The perspective of an outside authority.** In this case, data scientists from the University of Freiburg, made a huge difference to the lab's success. As Andreas Romer, ZF's Vice President for IT Innovation, put it, "We no longer consider innovation to be an internal process at ZF. To safeguard our future success, we must look beyond the confines of our company, build up partnerships to learn and also to share knowledge and experiences."

- **Domain experts.** While data scientists brought knowledge of analytic methods and approaches to the project, their access to domain experts was essential. Such experts need to be closely involved in answering domain-related questions that come up once the team is deeply engaged with the problem. In our experience, the capacity and availability of domain experts is the most common bottleneck blocking a data analytics project's progress.

Problems Solved

Three years on, we can say with confidence that the ZF Data Lab is a valuable addition to the company. With this dedicated resource, ZF has been able to solve problems that had stumped the company's engineers for years. Here are two examples:

- **Broken grinding rings.** A key source of stoppages in production line machinery, a breakdown can create a mess that may take hours to clean up. An internal client wanted to develop an early warning system that could indicate the probability of a future ring breakdown, but it had messy data, a weak signal (unclear data), and a highly unbalanced ground truth (because breakdowns happen only occasionally). Despite those limitations, we were able to create an algorithm that could detect imminent breaks 72% of the time—a far cry from five-decimal perfection but still enough to save the company thousands.

- **High-power demand charges.** Managing energy units to regulate energy demand at times of peak use is an effective way to reduce costs. Our goal was to develop an automated data-driven decision-making agent that provides action recommendations with the objective to lower load peaks. Working closely with the energy department, we were able to develop a working prediction model to avoid those high-demand surcharges. Following the model's recommendations should reduce the peak load by one to two megawatts, worth roughly $100,000–$200,000 per year.

After growing for three years, the ZF Data Lab has become a kind of specialized R&D function within the company. It is a melting pot of ideas and technologies, producing and evaluating proofs of concept, and discarding approaches that don't quite work. In the last analysis, the data lab is not only there to solve problems, but to help answer the biggest big data question of all: How will our company compete in this increasingly digital world?

TAKEAWAYS

ZF, a global automotive supplier based in Germany, feared a "Kodak moment," a fatal disruption that could redefine its business. So it set out to launch a dedicated lab that focused entirely on data challenges. Understanding how ZF set up and ran its analytics lab can help your organization to do the same.

✓ **Focus on the right internal customers.** Narrow your efforts to the departments in which data projects will have the most impact.

✓ **Identify high-impact problems.** Select the projects within those departments that have the highest-value outcomes. Consider three criteria: a clearly defined problem; data that is available, accessible, and good quality; and a motivated team.

✓ **Place a deadline on execution.** Limit the execution phase to three months, and give your team the right to cancel the project if necessary, so they can free up resources to use toward a better goal.

✓ **Consider other success factors.** Beyond these steps, ZF noted three additional ingredients in the lab's success: executive support, the perspective of an outside authority, and experts to answer domain-related questions once the team is engaged with a problem.

Adapted from content posted on hbr.org, November 2, 2018 (product #H04MRJ).

8

CLOUD COMPUTING IS HELPING SMALLER, NEWER FIRMS COMPETE

by Nicholas Bloom and Nicola Pierri

I s digital technology a democratizing force, allowing smaller, newer companies to compete against giant ones? Or does it provide even greater advantage to incumbents? That question has gotten a lot of attention lately, in response to data showing that the rate of new business creation in the United States has slowed, and that in most industries the biggest firms have higher market share than they did a decade ago.[1]

Despite those trends, our research suggests that technology can in fact provide an advantage to small and new firms. In recent research, we studied the adoption of cloud computing across U.S. businesses. Cloud computing is an IT paradigm based on remote access to a shared pool of computing resources. Putting data "in the cloud" essentially means paying someone else to manage it, and then connecting to their servers via the internet to access your data when you need it. It also means you don't need to analyze this data on your own machines but can "rent" these services on demand. The popularity of cloud computing has exploded during the last half decade. By cutting the fixed costs of computing—avoiding the need to hire IT staff, servers, and hardware—even the smallest firm can satisfy large and unexpected computing needs.

For example, KenSci is a small Seattle-based health care–analytics company, which uses machine-learning techniques to analyze hundreds of variables about patients' conditions to provide real-time predictions about mortality, readmissions, and other health-related risks. Relying on the cloud, KenSci has been able to quickly

We thank Toulouse Network for Information Technology for funding for the data.

scale up and offer its services worldwide, without building a sizable IT infrastructure beforehand. The computational agility of cloud computing has been playing a role in manufacturing as well, fostering the creation of new "smart'" products. Pivothead is a firm with 25 employees producing wearable technologies to help the blind and visually impaired. Information collected by the wearable sensors is sent to the cloud, processed through machine-learning algorithms, and transformed into speech or text, in order to help the client navigate the surrounding environment.

These anecdotes suggest that cloud computing has "democratized computing" by bringing it to the masses of firms. Our research confirms this intuition using a massive new data set of over one million U.S. firms since the 1980s. Specifically, we found three key results. First, cloud computing has seen massive growth. Less than 0.5% of firms had adopted it in 2010, whereas 7% had by 2016, which is an annualized growth rate of almost 50%. Second, the adoption of cloud computing has occurred across the United States, not just in one region—albeit with heaviest and earliest adoption in urban and educated areas. But third, and most strikingly, cloud computing—unlike other technologies like PCs and e-commerce—has been adopted first by smaller and younger firms.

The data set for our analysis comes from Aberdeen Information's call center, which has been making annual phone calls to millions of firms across the United States since the 1980s. It painstakingly records the hardware and software used by millions of firms per year back to 1981. This data set is often used by academic researchers because of its broad coverage and data quality. Surveys aren't perfect, of course, and one disadvantage of this data is that respondents have discretion over what they consider counts as cloud computing. (Although many internet services these days involve accessing your data from another company over the internet, for the purposes of this survey we expect that firms are responding to a narrower use case: the use of specific enterprise cloud-hosting services such as AWS, Microsoft Azure, Google Cloud Platform, IBM Cloud, Oracle, or Alibaba.) In this chapter we use the records from more than 150,000 U.S. firms with information on their adoption of cloud computing.

The Adoption of Cloud Technology Across Industries in the United States

Figure 8-1 shows the rise of cloud computing since 2010, the first year the database started recording it. We see cloud adoption rates rising from 0.3% in 2010 to 7% in 2016, which is a more than doubling every other year. Moreover, this rise has occurred in every broad industry

FIGURE 8-1

Cloud computing is becoming more common

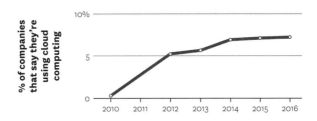

Note: 2011 data was not available.
Source: Aberdeen U.S. computing population files from 2010 to 2016

group we studied, highlighting how the increase in cloud computing has spanned the U.S. economy.

Our research also shows the geographic spread of cloud computing, showing a broad adoption across U.S. counties. This is not just a technology used by hipster startups in New York and San Francisco—it's being adopted all across the country. Every U.S. county we have data on has seen an increase in cloud computing since 2010.

Small, Young, and Cloudy

Our next chart is the most important. Figure 8-2 shows that the very smallest firms have the highest adoption rates. Firms with fewer than 25 employees have adoption rates of 10% to 15% on average, while medium-sized firms have lower adoption rates. Indeed, adoption rates are lowest in firms with about 100 employees, perhaps because they have enough scale to adopt in-house computing systems but not enough scale to be able to afford both those in-house systems and cloud services. The largest firms—those with 500 employees or more—again see rising adoption rates, typically with 5% to 10% of firms adopting cloud computing.

FIGURE 8-2

The smallest and largest companies are the heaviest adopters of cloud computing

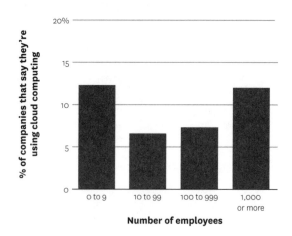

Number of employees

Source: Aberdeen U.S. computing population files, 2016

This cloud "tick" also turns out to be surprisingly robust. We see this across industries, firm types, and years in our data. Small firms really do seem to be the pioneers of cloud-computing adoption.

For contrast, we compared the adoption of cloud computing to adoption rates for two other technologies: personal computers (PCs) and e-commerce. These show the more classic pattern of greater adoption by large firms. Cloud really does stand out as being particularly attractive to the very smallest firms.

But it's not just small firms driving the adoption of cloud computing. Young firms are adopting cloud computing faster than older ones (see figure 8-3). So, the most nimble, youthful, and entrepreneurial companies are the pioneers of adoption. Again, we did not see that with other technologies—older firms tended to be the first adopters of PCs and e-commerce.

All of this suggests that cloud computing is an unusual technology that appeals to smaller, younger firms. We believe its ability to provide high-powered computing without the overhead costs associated with in-house software and hardware provision has driven this. In this sense cloud computing has spread computing out to the masses, democratizing computing.

Flexible access to computing resources allows small firms to scale up (or down) rapidly and to experiment

FIGURE 8-3

Younger companies are more likely to have adopted cloud computing

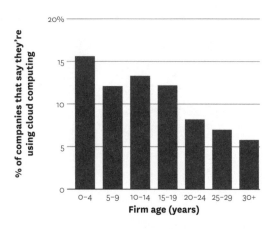

Source: Aberdeen U.S. computing population files, 2016

with new products and features. This operational agility can be particularly valuable when facing uncertain demand or a fast-evolving competitive environment. Recent evidence from the University of Toronto's Kristina McElheran and MIT's Wang Jin shows that the ability of "renting" IT resources has also aided young firms to survive and increase productivity.[2]

These are encouraging findings, especially in light of the decline in business dynamism and the rate of new startup creation documented by economics professor

John Haltiwanger and his colleagues.[3] Although we don't have data on how cloud computing affects firm performance, it's not hard to imagine that lowering computing costs would substantially improve younger and smaller companies' chances. Despite statistics suggesting a decline in U.S. dynamism, technology has been known to disrupt incumbents when they least expect it. Cloud computing may ultimately prove to be one of those disruptive forces.

TAKEAWAYS

The computational capacity to analyze big data sets comes with a price tag—one that smaller, newer companies may not be able to afford. They can compete by placing their computing efforts in the cloud.

✓ Putting data "in the cloud" means you're paying someone else to manage it, and you connect to their servers via the internet to access your data when you need it. Doing so means you don't need to analyze the data on your own machines but "rent" these services on demand, saving you the overhead costs of hiring IT staff or purchasing servers and hardware.

✓ Cloud computing has seen massive growth in recent years. Research indicates cloud adoption rates have increased drastically over the past decade across the United States.

✓ The smallest firms have the highest adoption rates. Younger firms, too, are adopting cloud computing faster than older ones.

✓ Flexible access to computing resources allows smaller firms to scale up or down quickly and experiment with new products and features. This agility is especially valuable when facing uncertain demand or a fast-evolving competitive environment.

NOTES

1. Ian Hathaway and Robert E. Litan, "Declining Business Dynamism in the United States: A Look at States and Metros," Brookings, May 5, 2014, https://www.brookings.edu/research/declining -business-dynamism-in-the-united-states-a-look-at-states-and -metros/; David Wessel, "Is Lack of Competition Strangling the U.S. Economy?" *Harvard Business Review*, March–April 2018, https://hbr.org/2018/03/is-lack-of-competition-strangling-the-u-s -economy.

2. Wang Jin and Kristina McElheran, "Economies Before Scale: Survival and Performance of Young Plants in the Age of Cloud Computing," Rotman School of Management Working Paper no. 3112901, December 2017.

3. Ryan A. Decker, John Haltiwanger, Ron S. Jarmin, and Javier Miranda, "Declining Business Dynamism: What We Know and the Way Forward," *American Economic Review* 106, no. 5 (May 2016).

Adapted from "Research: Cloud Computing Is Helping Smaller, Newer Firms Compete" on hbr.org, August 31, 2018 (product #H04ISD).

9

DATA SCIENCE AND THE ART OF PERSUASION

by Scott Berinato

Data science is growing up fast. Over the past five years companies have invested billions to get the most-talented data scientists to set up shop, amass zettabytes of material, and run it through their deduction machines to find signals in the unfathomable volume of noise. It's working—to a point. Data has begun to change our relationship to fields as varied as language translation, retail, health care, and basketball.

But despite the success stories, many companies aren't getting the value they could from data science. Even well-run operations that generate strong analysis fail to capitalize on their insights. Efforts fall short in the last mile, when it comes time to explain the stuff to decision makers.

In a question on Kaggle's 2017 survey of data scientists, to which more than 7,000 people responded, four of the top seven "barriers faced at work" were related to last-mile issues, not technical ones: "lack of management/ financial support," "lack of clear questions to answer," "results not used by decision makers," and "explaining data science to others." Those results are consistent with what the data scientist Hugo Bowne-Anderson found interviewing 35 data scientists for his podcast; as he wrote in a 2018 HBR.org article, "The vast majority of my guests tell [me] that the key skills for data scientists are . . . the abilities to learn on the fly and to communicate well in order to answer business questions, explaining complex results to nontechnical stakeholders."

In my work lecturing and consulting with large organizations on data visualization (dataviz) and persuasive presentations, I hear both data scientists and executives vent their frustration. Data teams know they're sitting on valuable insights but can't sell them. They say decision makers misunderstand or oversimplify their analysis and expect them to do magic, to provide the right answers to all their questions. Executives, meanwhile, complain about how much money they invest in data science operations that don't provide the guidance they hoped for. They don't see tangible results because the results aren't communicated in their language.

Gaps between business and technology types aren't new, but this divide runs deeper. Consider that 105 years ago, before coding and computers, Willard Brinton began his landmark book *Graphic Methods for Presenting Facts* by describing the last-mile problem: "Time after time it happens that some ignorant or presumptuous member of a committee or a board of directors will upset the carefully thought-out plan of a man who knows the facts, simply because the man with the facts cannot present his facts readily enough to overcome the opposition . . . As the cathedral is to its foundation so is an effective presentation of facts to the data."

How could this song remain the same for more than a century? Like anything else this deeply rooted, the last-mile problem's origins are multiple. For one, the tools used to do the science include visualization functionality. This encourages the notion that it's the responsibility of the data person to be the communicator. The default output of these tools can't match well-conceived, fully designed dataviz; their visualization often isn't as well developed as their data manipulation, and the people using the tools often don't want to do the communicating. Many data scientists have told me they're wary of visualization because it can dumb down their work and spur executives to draw conclusions that belie the nuance and uncertainty inherent in any scientific analysis. But in the rush to grab in-demand data scientists, organizations have been hiring the most technically oriented people they can find, ignoring their ability or desire (or lack thereof) to communicate with a lay audience.

That would be fine if those organizations also hired other people to close the gap—but they don't. They still expect data scientists to wrangle data, analyze it in the context of knowing the business and its strategy, make charts, and present them to a lay audience. That's unreasonable. That's unicorn stuff.

To begin solving the last-mile problem, companies must stop looking for unicorns and rethink what kind of talent makes up a data science operation. This chapter proposes a way for those who aren't getting the most out of their operations to free data scientists from unreasonable expectations and introduce new types of workers to the mix. It relies on cross-disciplinary teams composed of members with varying talents who work in close proximity. Empathy, developed through exposure to others' work, facilitates collaboration among the types of talent. Work is no longer passed between groups; it's shared among them.

A team approach—hardly new, but newly applied—can get data science operations over the last mile, delivering the value they've created for the organization.

Why Are Things Like This?

In the early 20th century, pioneers of modern management ran sophisticated operations for turning data into decisions through visual communication, and they did it with teams. It was a cross-disciplinary effort that included gang punch operators, card sorters, managers, and draftsmen (they were nearly always men). Examples of the results of this collaboration are legion in Brinton's book. Railroad companies and large manufacturers were especially adept, learning the most efficient routes to send materials through factories, achieving targets for regional sales performances, and even optimizing vacation schedules.

The team approach persisted through most of the century. In her 1969 book *Practical Charting Techniques,* Mary Eleanor Spear details the ideal team—a communicator, a graphic analyst, and a draftsman (still mostly men)—and its responsibilities. "It is advisable," Spear writes, "that [all three] collaborate."

In the 1970s things started to split. Scientists flocked to new technology that allowed them to visualize data in the same space (a computer program) where they manipulated it. Visuals were crude but available fast and required no help from anyone else. A crack opened in the dataviz world between computer-driven visualization and the more classic design-driven visualization produced by draftspeople (finally).

Chart Wizard, Microsoft's innovation in Excel, introduced "click and viz" for the rest of us, fully cleaving the two worlds. Suddenly anyone could instantly create a chart along with overwrought variations on it that made bars three-dimensional or turned a pie into a doughnut. The profoundness of this shift can't be overstated. It helped make charts a lingua franca for business. It fueled the use of data in operations and eventually allowed data science to exist, because it overcame the low limit on how much data human designers can process into visual communication. Most crucially, it changed the structure of work. Designers—draftspeople—were devalued and eventually fell out of data analysis. Visualization became the job of those who managed data, most of whom were neither trained to visualize nor inclined to learn. The speed and convenience of pasting a Chart Wizard graphic into a presentation prevailed over slower, more resource-intensive, design-driven visuals, even if the latter were demonstrably more effective.

With the advent of data science, the expectations put on data scientists have remained the same—do the work and communicate it—even as the requisite skills have broadened to include coding, statistics, and algorithmic modeling. Indeed, in HBR's landmark 2012 article on data scientist as the sexiest job of the 21st century, the role is described in explicitly unicornish terms: "What abilities make a data scientist successful? Think of him or her as a hybrid of data hacker, analyst, communicator, and trusted adviser. The combination is extremely powerful—and rare."

A rare combination of skills for the most sought-after jobs means that many organizations will be unable to recruit the talent they need. They will have to look for another way to succeed. The best way is to change the skill set they expect data scientists to have and rebuild teams with a combination of talents.

Building a Better Data Science Operation

An effective data operation based on teamwork can borrow from Brinton and Spear but will account for the modern context, including the volume of data being

How Communication Fails

I've learned in my work that most leaders recognize the value data science can deliver, and few are satisfied with how it's being delivered. Some data scientists complain that bosses don't understand what they do and underutilize them. Some managers complain that the scientists can't make their work intelligible to a lay audience.

In general, the stories I hear follow one of these scenarios. See if you recognize any of them.

The Statistician's Curse

A data scientist with vanguard algorithms and great data develops a suite of insights and presents them to decision makers in great detail. She believes that her analysis is objective and unassailable. Her charts are "click and viz" with some text added to the slides—in her view, design isn't something that serious statisticians spend time on. The language she uses in her presentation is unfamiliar to her listeners, who become confused and frustrated. Her analysis is dead-on, but her recommendation is not adopted.

(Continued)

The Factory and the Foreman

A business stakeholder wants to push through a pet project but has no data to back up his hypothesis. He asks the data science team to produce the analysis and charts for his presentation. The team knows that his hypothesis is ill formed, and it offers helpful ideas about a better way to approach the analysis, but he wants only charts and speaking notes. One of two things will happen: His meeting will be upended when someone asks about the data analysis and he can't provide answers, or his project will go through and then fail because the analysis was unsound.

The Convenient Truth

A top-notch information designer is inspired by some analysis from company data scientists and offers to help them create a beautiful presentation for the board, with on-brand colors and typography and engaging, easily accessible stories. But the scientists get nervous when the executives start to extract wrong ideas from the analysis. The clear, simple charts make certain relationships look like direct cause and effect when they're not, and they remove any uncertainty that's inherent in the analysis. The scientists are in a quandary: Finally, top decision makers are excited about their work, but what they're excited about isn't a good representation of it.

processed, the automation of systems, and advances in visualization techniques. It will also account for a wide range of project types, from the reasonably simple reporting of standard analytics data (say, financial results) to the most sophisticated big data efforts that use cutting-edge machine-learning algorithms.

Here are four steps to creating one:

1. Define talents, not team members

It might seem natural that the first step toward dismantling unicorn thinking is to assign various people to the roles the "perfect" data scientist now fills: data manipulator, data analyst, designer, and communicator.

Not quite. Rather than assign people to roles, define the talents you need to be successful. A talent is not a person; it's a skill that one or more people possess. One person may have several talents; three people may be able to handle five talents. It's a subtle distinction but an important one for keeping teams nimble enough to configure and reconfigure during various stages of a project. (We'll come back to this.)

Any company's list of talents will vary, but a good core set includes these six:

Project management. Because your team is going to be agile and will shift according to the type of project and how far along it is, strong PM employing some scrumlike methodology will run under every facet of the operation. A good project manager will have great organizational abilities and strong diplomacy skills, helping to bridge cultural gaps by bringing disparate talents together at meetings and getting all team members to speak the same language.

Data wrangling. Skills that compose this talent include building systems; finding, cleaning, and structuring data; and creating and maintaining algorithms and other statistical engines. People with wrangling talent will look for opportunities to streamline operations—for example, by building repeatable processes for multiple projects and templates for solid, predictable visual output that will jump-start the information-design process.

Data analysis. The ability to set hypotheses and test them, find meaning in data, and apply that to a specific business context is crucial—and, surprisingly, not as well represented in many data science operations as one might think. Some organizations are heavy on wranglers and rely on them to do the analysis as well. But good data analysis is separate from coding and math. Often this talent emerges not from computer science but from the liberal arts. The software company Tableau ranked the infusion of liberal arts into data analysis as one of the biggest trends in analytics in 2018. Critical thinking, context setting, and other aspects of learning in the humanities also happen to be core skills for analysis, data or otherwise. In an online lecture about the topic, the Tableau research scientist Michael Correll explained why he thinks infusing data science with liberal arts is crucial. "It's impossible to consider data divorced from people," he says. "Liberal arts is good at helping us step in and see context. It makes people visible in a way they maybe aren't in the technology."

Subject expertise. It's time to retire the trope that data science teams are stuck in the basement to do their arcane work and surface only when the business needs something from them. Data science shouldn't be thought of as a service unit; it should have management talent on the team. People with knowledge of the business and the strategy will inform project design and data analysis and keep the team focused on business outcomes, not just on building the best statistical models. Joaquin Candela, who runs applied machine learning at Facebook, has worked hard to focus his team on business outcomes and to reward decisions that favor those outcomes over improving data science.

Design. This talent is widely misunderstood. Good design isn't just choosing colors and fonts or coming up with an aesthetic for charts. That's styling—part of design, but by no means the most important part. Rather, people with design talent develop and execute systems for effective visual communication. In our context, they understand how to create and edit visuals to focus an audience and distill ideas. Information-design talent—which emphasizes understanding and manipulating data visualization— is ideal for a data science team.

Storytelling. Narrative is an extremely powerful human contrivance and one of the most underutilized in data science. The ability to present data insights as a story will, more than anything else, help close the communication gap between algorithms and executives. "Storytelling with data," a tired buzz phrase, is widely misunderstood, though. It is decidedly not about turning presenters into Stephen Kings or Tom Clancys. Rather, it's about understanding the structure and mechanics of narrative and applying them to dataviz and presentations.

TABLE 9-1

Core talents for communicating data

Here are the ways that various talents are involved as a data science project proceeds from gathering data to developing insight to presenting to stakeholders.

Talent	Tasks	Skills	Leads	Supports
Project management	• Manage creation of team, timeline, and schedules • Marshal resources • Troubleshoot	• Organization • Methodology (such as scrum) • People management	• During creation of a data science operation • During creation and execution of a project	• Ongoing data science operations
Data wrangling	• Find, clean, and structure data • Develop and implement data and visualization systems, algorithms, and models • Develop templates and systems for repeatable processes	• Coding • Statistics • Systems architecture	• Early in a data team's existence • Early in a project's development	• During routine data analysis, hypothesis testing, and visual exploration of data

Data analysis	• Develop and test hypotheses on data and data models • Find patterns and useful trends to inform business decisions	• Statistics • Scientific method • Critical thinking • Technical and nontechnical communication	• During routine data analysis, project design, hypothesis testing, and visual exploration of data	• Early in a data team's existence • Early in project development • During visual communication development and presentations to lay audiences
Subject expertise	• Define business goals • Develop and test hypotheses • Develop nontechnical communication	• Functional knowledge • Critical thinking • Strategy development • Nontechnical communication	• During project design, hypothesis testing, and visual exploration of data • During communication to nontechnical audiences	• Early in a data team's existence • During visualization and design process
Design	• Develop visual communication and presentations • Create templates and styles for repeatable visualization	• Information design • Presentation design • Design thinking • Persuasive communication	• During data visualization and the creation of presentations and visual systems (templating)	• During visual iteration and prototyping
Storytelling	• Develop stories from data and visuals • Help construct presentations in story format • Present to nontechnical audiences	• Information design • Writing and editing • Presenting • Persuasive communication	• During creation of data visualization and presentations • During presentation to nontechnical audiences	• During visual iteration and prototyping

2. Hire to create a portfolio of necessary talents

Once you've identified the talents you need, free your recruiting from the idea that these are roles you should hire people to fill. Instead focus on making sure these talents are available on the team. Some of them naturally tend to go together: Design and storytelling, for example, or data wrangling and data analysis, may exist in one person.

Sometimes the talent will be found not in employees but in contractors. For my work, I keep a kitchen cabinet of people who have talents in areas where I'm weak. You may want to engage an information-design firm, or contract with some data wranglers to clean and structure new data streams.

Thinking of talents as separate from people will help companies address the last-mile problem, because it will free them from trying to find the person who can both do data science and communicate it. Nabbing some people who have superior design skills will free data scientists to focus on their strengths. It will also open the door to people who might previously have been ignored. An average coder who also has good design skills, for example, might be very useful.

Randal Olson, the lead data scientist at Life Epigenetics and curator of the Reddit channel Data Is Beautiful (devoted to sharing and discussing good dataviz), used to focus solely on how well someone did the technical part of data science. "I know, when I started, I had zero appreciation for the communication part of it," he says. "I think that's common." Now, in some cases, he has changed the hiring process. "You know, they come in and we immediately start white-boarding models and math," he says. "It's data scientists talking to data scientists. Now I will sometimes bring in a nontechnical person and say to the candidate, 'Explain this model to this person.'"

3. Expose team members to talents they don't have

Overcoming culture clashes begins with understanding others' experiences. Design talent often has no exposure to statistics or algorithms. Its focus is on aesthetic refinement, simplicity, clarity, and narrative. The depth and complexity of data work is hard for designers to reconcile. Hard-core data scientists, in contrast, value objectivity, statistical rigor, and comprehensiveness; the communication part is not only foreign to them but distracting. "It goes against their ethos," says one manager of a data science operation at a large tech company. "I was the same way, working in data science for 10 years, but it was eye-opening for me when I had to build a team. I

FIGURE 9-1

Build a talent dashboard

Performing a talent audit helps managers do a better job of planning for projects and configuring teams.

First, identify the talents you need to have access to:

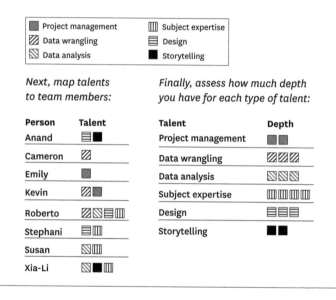

Next, map talents to team members:

Finally, assess how much depth you have for each type of talent:

saw that if we just learned a little more about the communication part of it, we could champion so much more for the business."

There are many ways to expose team members to the value of others' talents. Designers should learn some basic statistics—take an introductory course, for example—

FIGURE 9-2

Put it to use

Knowing what talents are available, managers can now assign units of talent to a project according to when it's needed. Typically, one cluster of talents will take the lead early in a project, and different clusters will do so in the later stages. Project management usually plays a big role throughout.

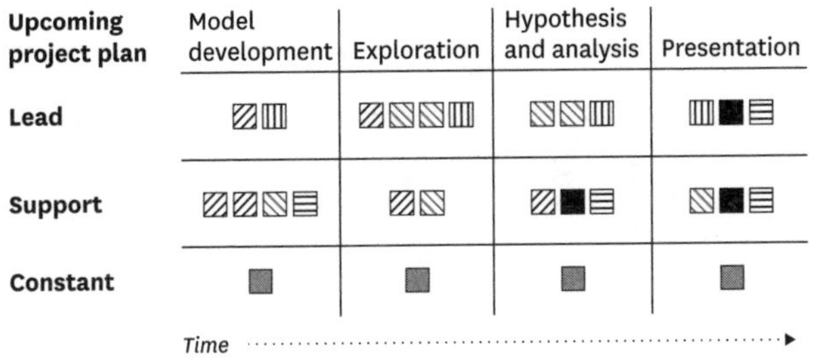

Upcoming project plan	Model development	Exploration	Hypothesis and analysis	Presentation
Lead	▧▥	▧▨▨▥	▨▨▥	▥■☰
Support	▧▧▨☰	▧▨	▧■☰	▨■☰
Constant	▦	▦	▦	▦

Time ···➤

while data scientists learn basic design principles. Neither must become experts in their counterparts' field—they just need to learn enough to appreciate each other.

Stand-ups and other meetings should always include a mix of talents. A scrum stand-up geared mostly to updating on tech progress can still include a marketer who makes presentations, as happens at Olson's company. Subject-matter experts should bring data-wrangling and analysis talent to strategy meetings. Special sessions at which stakeholders answer questions from the data team and vice versa also help to bridge the gap. The chief algorithms officer at Stitch Fix, Eric Colson (who is something close to a unicorn, having both statistical and communication talents at a company where data science is intrinsic), asks his team members to make one-minute presentations to nontechnical audiences, forcing them to frame problems in smart ways that everyone can understand. "To this day," Colson says, "if you say 'coconuts' here, people will know that was part of a metaphor one person used to describe a particular statistical problem he was tackling. We focus on framing it in ways everyone understands because the business won't do what it doesn't understand." Another manager of a data science team created a glossary of terms used by technical talent and design talent to help employees become familiar with one another's language.

If your organization contains some of those rare people who, like Colson, have both data talents and communication and design talents, it helps to have them mentor one another. People who express interest in developing talents that they don't have but that you need should be encouraged, even if those strengths (design skills, say) are far afield from the ones they already have (data wrangling). Indeed, in my workshops I hear from data scientists who would love to develop their design or storytelling talent but don't have time to commit to it. Others would love to see that talent added to their teams, but their project management focuses primarily on technical outcomes, not business ones.

All this exposure is meant to create empathy among team members with differing talents. Empathy in turn creates trust, a necessary basis for effective teamwork. Colson recalls a time he used storytelling talent to help explain something coming out of data analysis: "I remember doing a presentation on a merchandising problem, where I thought we were approaching it the wrong way. I had to get merchandising to buy in." Instead of explaining beta-binomial distribution and other statistical concepts to bolster his point of view, he told a story about someone pulling balls from an urn and what happened over time to the number and type of balls in the urn. "People loved it," he says. "You watched the room and how it clicked with them and gave them confidence so that at that point the math behind it wasn't even necessary to explain. They trusted us."

4. Structure projects around talents

With a portfolio of talents in place, it's time to use it to accomplish your goals. The shifting nature of what talents are needed and when can make projects unwieldy. Strong project management skills and experience in agile methodologies will help in planning the configuration and reconfiguration of talents, marshaling resources as needed, and keeping schedules from overwhelming any part of the process.

Putting It All Together

You'll want to take other steps to make your projects successful:

Assign a single, empowered stakeholder

It's possible, or even likely, that not all the people whose talents you need will report to the data science team manager. Design talent may report to marketing; subject-matter experts may be executives reporting to the CEO. Nevertheless, it's important to give the team as much decision-making power as possible. Stakeholders will most often be people with business expertise who are closely connected to or responsible for business goals; the aim of the work, after all, is better business outcomes. Those people can create shared goals and incentives for the team. Ideally you can avoid the responsibility-without-authority trap, in which the team is dealing with several stakeholders who may not all be aligned.

Assign leading talent and support talent

Who leads and who supports will depend on what kind of project it is and what phase it's in. For example, in a deeply exploratory project, in which large volumes of data are being processed and visualized just to find patterns, data wrangling and analysis take the lead, with support from subject expertise; design talent may not participate at all, since no external communication is required. Conversely, to prepare a report for the board on evidence for a recommended strategy adjustment, storytelling and design lead with support from data talent.

Colocate

Have all team members work in the same physical space during a project. Also set up a shared virtual space for communication and collaboration. It would be undesirable to have those with design and storytelling talent using a Slack channel while the tech team is using GitHub and the business experts are collaborating over email. Use "paired analysis" techniques, whereby team members literally sit next to each other and work on one screen in a scrumlike iterative process. They may be people with data-wrangling and analysis talent refining data models and testing hypotheses, or a pair with both subject expertise and storytelling ability who are working together to polish a presentation, calling in design when they have to adapt a chart.

Make it a real team

The crucial conceit in colocation is that it's one empowered team. At Stitch Fix "our rule is no handoffs," Colson says. "We don't want to have to coordinate three people across departments." To this end he has made it a priority to ensure that his teams have all the skills they need to accomplish their goals with limited external support. He also tries to hire people many would consider generalists who cross the tech-communication gap. He augments this model with regular feedback for, say, a data person who needs help with storytelling, or a subject expert who needs to understand some statistical principle.

Reuse and template

Colson also created an "algo UI team." Think of this as a group of people who combine their design talents and data-wrangling talents to create reusable code sets for producing good dataviz for the project teams. Such templates are invaluable for getting a team operating efficiently. Conversations that an information designer, say, would have with a data analyst about best practices in visualization become hard-coded in the tools. Graham MacDonald, the chief data scientist at the Urban Institute, has successfully fostered this kind of cooperation on templating. His group produces data by county for many U.S. counties. By getting data wrangling and subject expertise together to understand the communication needs, the group built a reusable template that could customize the output for any particular county. Such an outcome would have been difficult without the integration of those talents on the team.

Conclusion

The presentation of data science to lay audiences—the last mile—hasn't evolved as rapidly or as fully as the science's technical part. It must catch up, and that means rethinking how data science teams are put together, how they're managed, and who's involved at every point in the process, from the first data stream to the final chart shown to the board. Until companies can successfully traverse that last mile, data science teams will underdeliver. They will provide, in Willard Brinton's words, foundations without cathedrals.

TAKEAWAYS

Companies responded to the analytics boom by hiring the best data scientists, but many of them haven't gotten the value they expected from their data science initiatives. Their efforts fall short when it comes to communicating their findings to decision makers—otherwise known as the last-mile problem.

- ✓ Companies must rethink how they build their data science teams by focusing on six talents: project management, data wrangling, data analysis, subject expertise, design, and storytelling.

- ✓ Identify which of these talents are missing on your team. Find a variety of people who have these skills to fill these gaps, remembering that some may excel in more than one.

✓ Expose team members to the value of others' talents to prevent culture clashes. If one individual excels in design and another in analysis, encourage them to learn each other's skills, so they can appreciate what other team members bring to the table.

✓ Use these talents to accomplish your goals by structuring your projects around these skills.

Reprinted from Harvard Business Review, *January–February 2019 (product #R1901K).*

Section 3

APPLYING DATA ANALYTICS

10

HOW VINEYARD VINES USES ANALYTICS TO WIN OVER CUSTOMERS

by Dave Sutton

When brothers Shep and Ian Murray cut their ties with corporate America to start a little company on Martha's Vineyard in 1998, their motivation was clear: "We're making neckties so we don't have to wear them."[1]

Little did they know that the business they founded, Vineyard Vines, would become a darling of the fashion industry and a household brand name around the country.

Today, the company best known for its smiling pink whale logo offers much more than its signature neckwear. It manufactures a full line of "exclusive, yet attainable" clothing and accessories for men, women, and children. That "little" privately held business has grown tremendously since its launch and currently has more than 90 physical retail locations and a highly successful e-commerce business.

I met the team at Vineyard Vines while doing research about data-driven marketing technologies for my book, *Marketing, Interrupted*, and learned firsthand about the company's beginnings and what has made it so successful today. From the very beginning, the Murray brothers adopted a guiding principle to authentically connect with and deeply understand the unique needs of their customers. This principle has always been a priority for the leadership team at Vineyard Vines and it is still top of mind today. It is clear that the current VP of Marketing, Lindsey Worster, is committed to this principle, as she told me: "We are all about getting the right message, about the right product, at the right time to our customer—targeted, relevant, and authentic communication is our primary goal."

Of course, this type of real-time, one-to-one marketing is easier said than done.

As Vineyard Vines has rapidly grown its customer base, the size of its customer database has expanded, too. Terabytes of data have been captured. Hundreds of attributes, encompassing customer profiles, preferences, and buying behaviors, must be parsed into actionable insights in order to deliver a highly personalized experience. Like many competitors in the apparel industry, Vineyard Vines has kept its operations lean in order to preserve operating margins. This means that it simply does not have the human resources to perform the onerous data analysis and behavioral segmentation needed to inform true one-to-one marketing. So, over the years, the retailer fell into the trap of relying on traditional "batch-and-blast" types of communications to reach its customers, promote products, and make offers. Of course, that trade-off was inconsistent with the guiding principles of the founders, but it was perceived to be the only way to keep the cash register ringing. But, Worster acknowledged, "With the batch-and-blast campaigns, we were sending the exact same message and static images to millions of people, and that just isn't the best way to communicate with customers."

In July 2016, the e-commerce team at Vineyard Vines set out to find a solution to help it keep pace with its dynamic customer base and stay true to its principles of authentic, relevant, and personalized communications. What team members were looking for was a retailer-agnostic platform that would integrate their online customer and products data to enable true one-to-one, personalized messaging. As we all know, Amazon has the technology to do this, but it's proprietary and not available to retailers.

Enter Fayez Mohamood and his team at Bluecore, a retail marketing automation platform. The solution that Fayez and his team have developed correlates customer behaviors and their interactions with the retailer's online product catalog. From these analytics, Bluecore dynamically builds intelligent, triggered campaigns that can be run across email and social media channels or be used to optimize search-engine marketing. At the heart of the solution sits an AI-driven decisioning engine that determines the timing and content of the next best campaign to send to individual shoppers. The decisioning engine takes the data about the customers' interactions with specific products and decides what products to target next for each customer, based on its understanding of the individual and the collective wisdom of all customers. It understands which customers have price sensitivities (and therefore are motivated by discounts), what items an individual customer has viewed, what those items have in common with other items the customer engaged with, which products are replenishable items and at what cadence a specific customer replenishes them, which activities predict an upcoming purchase, the right time to contact a specific customer, a customers' lifetime value and activity, and so on.

Initially, Vineyard Vines deployed the technology to tackle obvious challenges like triggering emails for abandoned shopping carts, abandoned searches, and abandoned browses. After seeing increases in revenue per email (RPE) on those initial customer messaging efforts, the marketing team decided to expand its use of the dynamic decisioning capabilities of the platform—what Bluecore refers to as "predictive audiences." This part of the platform enables Vineyard Vines to send dynamic, personalized messaging based on a customer's online behaviors, purchase transactions, and their relative level of personal engagement with the brand.

Next, the marketing team quickly set about using the platform to automate campaigns for specific use cases where personalization and relevancy had always been a challenge, including:

- notifying customers when high-demand products were back in stock

- communicating last-chance offers on stock-out items

- running holiday-specific and special event campaigns

- predicting when a customer may be at risk of unsubscribing

The days of batch-and-blast campaigns for Vineyards Vines may soon be over, as to date the campaign results with the new decisioning engine have been exceeding expectations. Consider the following campaign examples:

Holiday campaigns expand reach without sacrificing relevance

The Vineyard Vines team increased the reach for its annual St. Patrick's Day email campaign from 3,000 recipients in 2017 to more than 239,000 in 2018, while maintaining a highly personalized approach. This holiday-themed product campaign targeted two specific audiences: customers who had previously viewed the holiday-themed apparel and customers with a high affinity toward the product. The open rate for emails generated from the new platform was up 68% and the RPE increased by 572% over the prior year, when a batch-and-blast approach had been used. For the annual Easter campaign, the marketing team used the platform to target not only customers who had browsed

Easter-related products previously but also expanded the list of recipients to include customers who had a high affinity toward the products. In this case, the number of recipients jumped from 5,000 to 150,000, open rates were up 77%, and RPE was up 759% over the prior year's results.

A seasonal campaign generates outsized ROI through enhanced cross-channel marketing

The social media team at Vineyard Vines used the decisioning engine to determine which customers are unlikely to open or click emails and then targeted those customers on Facebook instead. This cross-channel move resulted in a 182% ROI. Based on its initial success, the team plans to extend this approach to even more channels. First up is an anti-churn campaign that targets at-risk customers through direct mail. The team believes this campaign will offer a powerful opportunity to reengage with these customers in a new way.

A women's performance campaign far outperforms expectations

The goal of this campaign was to introduce a new women's performance collection to customers who would have a high affinity for the product line based on predictive models. Since this was a brand-new product launch, the team didn't have any historical purchase behavior to use as a guide for segmentation, so Bluecore was used to close that gap. The target audience was customers who had a high or very high product affinity for Vineyard Vines's brand-new women's performance leggings. Using the new decisioning engine, the campaign generated 124% higher RPE than the average Vineyard Vines women's campaign.

The decisioning engine helps find new customer segments

The Vineyard Vines team is using the "audience insights" module of Bluecore to reveal retail-focused insights for specific groups of customers. In terms of customer needs, the ability to map customers to different life cycle stages helped the Vineyard Vines team home in on which priority customers to target, such as those who are at risk of opting out of direct marketing communications and losing touch with the brand. Looking at engagement with products, the team found "hidden gems," or products with low traffic but high conversion rates. This insight clued the team in on the products to which they should drive more traffic through targeted campaigns. When the marketing team combined the intelligence from audience insights with predictive decisioning, the results were impressive. For example, after finding that several kids' products landed in the "hidden gems" category, the team decided to create a "Kids' Weekly Best Sellers" campaign to drive more traffic to those products. It targeted customers who had previously browsed kids' products, had a high-to-medium likelihood of opening emails, and were unlikely to unsubscribe. Within the first 24 hours, the campaign brought in an 81% higher revenue per email than the traditional batch-and-blast kids' email campaigns.

What can other companies learn from Vineyard Vines's success? A few best practices stand out:

- Engage with customers on a one-to-one level. It's no longer a "nice-to-have"—customers expect it.

- Overhaul your batch-and-blast approach to email marketing by integrating behavioral data and predictive algorithms to make high-volume campaign sends that are unique to each recipient.

- Provide your loyal customers with the best experience at every touchpoint.

- Target customers in a personalized manner across more than just email, and determine the best channel mix for each customer.

- Gain a deeper understanding of customers and products. View detailed audience insights to better understand customer health and engagement with products.

Without tools like Bluecore, retailers don't have a clear or accessible understanding of what products customers are interacting with or the commonalities across products that a single customer has engaged with. They also don't know the minute that a product's status changes. Consider the occasions when a product decreases in value, goes out of stock, or is back in stock again—all of these events should trigger action by the retailer. Most retailers struggle to understand how and why a customer engages with a product unless the customer buys it or abandons the cart. Today, there's so much more that can be done to better serve customers and to ultimately make your company more successful.

TAKEAWAYS

Vineyard Vines uses its customers' data to connect with them authentically using real-time, one-to-one marketing.

Understanding what this company has learned through its analytics and AI efforts can help you improve your marketing campaigns to reengage customers and increase revenue.

✓ Moving past batch-and-blast messages that sent the same text and images to millions, Vineyard Vines looked to authentic, relevant, and personalized communications through a retail marketing automation platform. This platform created triggered campaigns based on an AI-driven decisioning engine that determined the timing and content delivered for each shopper.

✓ The company also expanded into "predictive audiences," which enabled the company to send personalized messages based on the customers' online behaviors, purchase transactions, and level of personal engagement with the brand.

✓ The Vineyard Vines example illuminates a few additional best practices: Provide your customers with the best experiences at every touchpoint; determine the best channel mix for each customer; and view detailed audience insights to understand customer health and engagement with products.

NOTE

1. Ray A. Smith, "Tie Association, a Fashion Victim, Calls It Quits as Trends Change," *Wall Street Journal*, June 4, 2008, https://www.wsj.com/articles/SB121253690573743197.

Adapted from content posted on hbr.org, June 8, 2018 (product #H04DRC).

HOW TO USE EMPLOYEE DATA RESPONSIBLY

by Ellyn Shook, Eva Sage-Gavin, and Susan Cantrell

I n the wake of recent customer data breaches, companies are recognizing the need for more protections and transparency around the collection and use of customer data. But few have paid equal attention to the issues arising from the collection and mining of *workplace* data.

Companies have vast amounts of valuable data on work and their workforce, and executives recognize the opportunity to use this data to improve productivity and to motivate and engage people. But employees are skeptical.

We surveyed more than 10,000 workers, across all skill levels and generations, and 1,400 C-level executives, in 13 countries and 13 industries. We found that more than 90% of the employees are willing to let their employers collect and use data on them and their work, but *only if* they benefit in some way.[1] And they harbor serious concerns about how companies might use the data. Perhaps for good reason: Only 30% of the executives whose companies use workforce data reported being highly confident they are using the data responsibly.

There's a great deal at stake in misusing employees' data. Our survey measured how employee trust increases or decreases in relation to 31 workforce data practices, and then we created an economic model to determine the effect of trust levels on revenue. We found that businesses risk losing 6% of current revenue growth if they lose the trust of their people. On the other side, higher trust, or a "trust dividend," would be worth more than a 6% increase in revenue growth.

How can companies use workplace data in an effective, responsible, and ethical way? Our research suggests a framework of three key actions responsible leaders can take.

Give Employees More Control

Consumers have become highly conscious of how their personal data is used and misused. And they have been supported by new laws and regulations that give them more control over their data. But this isn't the case in the workplace.

Protections of people's work-related data are still years behind that of consumer-related data, and the governance of workforce data skews heavily toward the corporation. If leaders want access to valuable data, they will need to forge a new "give and get" relationship with employees and share more control with them over their own data.

For example, wall-mounted cameras track every person and asset at our client Schlumberger's Center for Reliability & Efficiency in Denton, Texas, a facility that carries out maintenance and manufacturing of oil field equipment. The video data is aggregated and anonymized, and AI analyzes patterns to improve productivity. The data is never used to monitor how individuals work, but anyone can opt in privately to see their own performance data. This has its benefits: For example, the company drew on the data to grant workers more frequent but shorter breaks to combat productivity-sapping fatigue.

One step toward giving employees more control would be to create a single place where they can see, manage, and even delete the data their employer has collected about them. For instance, our client Telstra, Australia's largest telecommunications company, maintains an internal site called MyCareer that allows workers to keep and update their own career data and even challenge any incorrect or incomplete inputs.

Create a System of Checks and Balances

Governing the collection and use of massive quantities of sensitive data is fraught with risk. Companies need a system that builds in the right checks and balances.

Ideally, a C-level executive would be accountable for ensuring that workplace data and technologies are used in a responsible and ethical way. But less than 20% of the companies captured in our survey have a C-level executive in charge of this today, although another 48% reported having plans to change that soon. Some companies are even creating new roles, such as the chief ethics officer or chief data officer, to assume this responsibility.

But because the issues are so complex, the appointed leader must be supported by an executive-level coalition. That's why JPMorgan Chase brings together three members of the C-suite—human resources, risk, and legal. As Chief Human Resources Officer Robin Leopold told us, these leaders "come together to thoughtfully consider how we balance data insights for business benefit and respect for individuals' privacy—looking through the lens of strategic business resiliency, risk, and the ability to elevate our people."

Getting employees involved in these efforts to better monitor workplace data and technology is also important. When employees are asked for their input into how systems are designed and used, companies can avoid doing unintended harm.

Use Data to Elevate People, Not Penalize Them

By using new technologies and the resulting data responsibly, companies can unlock the potential of their people and preempt fears of "digital determinism"—the idea that tech will determine social structures, cultural values, and one's own experiences.

To uphold this responsibility, companies need to get creative. For example, AXA, a French multinational insurance firm we work with, has recently developed a virtual career assistant that uses AI algorithms to track the skills and interests of employees. It answers questions employees have about their careers, such as: Will a robot do my job? What other job options are there for me? What's the best training for me? AXA is now working on an extension that will match a person's values and traits with corporate culture to ensure employees are in the right work environment.

Companies can also use technology to track employee performance, both for good (to raise performance) or for ill (to penalize people). Many companies now track people—to see, for example, how fast they are working—and share real-time results on scorecards or in a live gaming format. But this can lead employees to feel that their every move is being watched. This real-time monitoring can raise worker stress, lower job satisfaction, and increase turnover.

But when the motivation is to help people get better at what they do, tracking employees can be beneficial. At AdventHealth Celebration (formerly Florida Hospital Celebration Health), nurses and patient-care technicians wear badges embedded with sensors, which track where they go during their shift, showing how often they visit patients' rooms or the nurses' station. According to the organization, they haven't used this data for punitive reasons, and the smart sensors have helped improve supply-stocking procedures and made nurses' shifts more efficient and their jobs easier.

Companies must also use technology creatively to reduce bias in hiring and promotion. While algorithms can be biased too, smart machines can reduce subjectivity and help managers make fairer decisions. In speaking with industry experts, we learned about one multinational financial services company that used an AI-powered recruiting tool to increase female applicants for financial roles by 150% and female applicants for all positions by 39%. Candidates' cognitive and social traits are measured as they play neuroscience-based games—providing leaders with the science-backed data predictive of performance to make better and less-biased hiring decisions.

Managing the Privacy-Performance Trade-Off

The emergence of AI and other smart technologies in the workplace calls for trade-offs between privacy and performance. Data can unlock people's potential and boost business performance, but these aren't prizes worth having if they diminish fairness and trust. Leaders must ask themselves: Just because we can, does it always mean we should?

C-suite leaders have to put trust at the heart of business strategy, on equal footing with growth and profitability, as trust is the ultimate currency of the digital age.

TAKEAWAYS

More and more, companies are gathering and analyzing data about how their employees work to improve productivity and motivate their people. But employees harbor serious concerns about how this data will be used. Companies must use this information responsibly and ethically to maintain employee trust.

✓ Give your people more control by allowing them to opt in to having their data collected, and provide a place where they can see, manage, and even delete their data.

✓ Establish a system of checks and balances by appointing a leader to monitor the use of workplace data. Keep employees involved in these efforts.

✓ Use the data as motivation or for recognition, rather than as evidence for punishment. This will help avoid the feeling that employees are being watched to see when they'll make mistakes. Use this data, too, to help sidestep human bias when it comes to hiring and promotion.

✓ People's work-related data is not yet regulated or protected—it is up to companies to ensure that they are using it safely and ethically. Ask yourself, "Just because we can collect this data, does it always mean we should?"

NOTE

1. Ellyn Shook, Mark Knickrehm, and Eva Sage-Gavin, "Decoding Organizational DNA," Accenture, https://www.accenture.com /us-en/insights/future-workforce/workforce-data-organizational -dna.

Adapted from "How Companies Can Use Employee Data Responsibly" on hbr.org, February 15, 2019 (product #H04T19).

12

WHAT AI-DRIVEN DECISION MAKING LOOKS LIKE

by Eric Colson

Many companies have adapted to a "data-driven" approach for operational decision making. Data can improve decisions, but it requires the right processor to get the most from it. Many people assume that processor is human. The term "data-driven" even implies that data is curated by—and summarized for— people to process.

But to fully leverage the value contained in data, companies need to bring artificial intelligence into their workflows and, sometimes, get us humans out of the way. We need to evolve from data-driven to AI-driven workflows.

Distinguishing between "data-driven" and "AI-driven" isn't just semantics. Each term reflects different assets, the former focusing on data and the latter processing ability. Data holds the insights that can enable better decisions; processing is the way to extract those insights and take actions. Humans and AI are both processors, with very different abilities. To understand how best to leverage each it's helpful to review our own biological evolution and how decision making has evolved in industry.

Just 50 to 75 years ago human judgment was the central processor of business decision making (see figure 12-1). Professionals relied on their highly tuned intuitions, developed from years of experience (and a relatively tiny bit of data) in their domain, to, say, pick the right creative for an ad campaign, determine the right inventory levels to stock, or approve the right financial investments. Experience and gut instinct were most of what was available to discern good from bad, high from low, and risky from safe.

It was, perhaps, all too human. Our intuitions are far from ideal decision-making instruments. Our brains

FIGURE 12-1

A decision-making model based on human judgment

are inflicted with many cognitive biases that impair our judgment in predictable ways. This is the result of hundreds of thousands of years of evolution where, as early hunter-gatherers, we developed a system of reasoning that relies on simple heuristics—shortcuts or rules of thumb that circumvent the high cost of processing a lot of information. This enabled quick, almost unconscious decisions to get us out of potentially perilous situations. However, "quick and almost unconscious" didn't always mean optimal or even accurate.

Imagine a group of our hunter-gatherer ancestors huddled around a campfire when a nearby bush suddenly rustles. A decision of the "quick and almost unconscious" type needs to be made: Conclude that the rustling is a dangerous predator and flee, or gather more information to see if it is potential prey—say, a rabbit, which could provide rich nutrients. Our more impulsive ancestors— those who decided to flee—survived at a higher rate than their more inquisitive peers. The cost of flight and losing out on a rabbit was far lower than the cost of sticking around and risking loss of one's own life to a predator. With such asymmetry in outcomes, evolution favors the trait that leads to less costly consequences, even at the sacrifice of accuracy. Therefore, the trait for more impulsive decision making and less information processing becomes prevalent in the descendant population.

In modern context, survival heuristics become myriad cognitive biases preloaded in our inherited brains. These biases influence our judgment and decision making in ways that depart from rational objectivity. We give more weight than we should to vivid or recent events. We coarsely classify subjects into broad stereotypes that don't sufficiently explain their differences. We anchor on prior experience even when it is completely irrelevant. We tend to conjure up specious explanations for events that are really just random noise. These are just a few of the dozens of ways cognitive bias plagues human judgment, a bias that for many decades was the central processor of business decision making. We know now that human intuition is inefficient, capricious, and fallible, and relying solely on it limits the ability of the organization.

Data-Supported Decision Making

Thank goodness, then, for data. Connected devices now capture unthinkable volumes of data: every transaction, every customer gesture, every micro- and macro-economic indicator, all the information that can inform better decisions. In response to this new data-rich environment we've adapted our workflows. IT departments support the flow of information using machines (databases, distributed file systems, and the like) to reduce the unmanageable volumes of data down to digestible summaries for human consumption. The summaries are then further processed by humans using tools like spreadsheets, dashboards, and analytics applications. Eventually, the highly processed, and now manageably small, data is presented for decision making. This is the "data-driven" workflow, as shown in figure 12-2. Human judgment is still the central processor, but now it uses summarized data as a new input.

While it's undoubtedly better than relying solely on intuition, humans playing the role of central processor still suffer from several limitations:

1. We don't leverage all the data. Summarized data can obscure many of the insights, relationships,

FIGURE 12-2

A decision-making model that utilizes summarized data

and patterns contained in the original (big) data set. Data reduction is necessary to accommodate the throughput of human processors. For as much as we are adept at digesting our surroundings, effortlessly processing vast amounts of ambient information, we are remarkably limited when it comes to processing the structured data manifested as millions or billions of records. The mind can handle sales numbers and average selling price rolled up to a regional level. It struggles or shuts down once you start to think about the full distribution of values and, crucially, the relationships between data elements—information lost in aggregate summaries but important to good decision making. (This is not to suggest that data summaries are not useful. To be sure, they are great at providing basic visibility into the business. But they will provide little value for use in decision making. Too much is lost in the preparation for humans.) In other cases, summarized data can be outright misleading. Confounding factors can give the appearance of a positive relationship when it is actually the opposite (see Simpson's and other paradoxes). And once data is aggregated, it may be impossible to recover contributing factors in order to properly control for them. (The best practice is to use randomized controlled trials, that is, A/B testing. Without this practice, even AI may not be able to properly control for confounding factors.) In short, by using humans as central processors of data, we are still trading off accuracy to circumvent the high cost of human data processing.

2. Data is not enough to insulate us from cognitive bias. Data summaries are directed by humans in a way that is prone to all those cognitive biases. We direct the summarization in a manner that is intuitive to us. We ask that the data be aggregated into segments that we feel are representative archetypes. Yet, we have that tendency to coarsely classify subjects into broad stereotypes that don't sufficiently explain their differences. For example, we may roll up the data to attributes such as geography even

when there is no discernible difference in behavior between regions. Summaries also can be thought of as a "coarse grain," or rougher approximation, of the data. For instance, an attribute like geography needs to be kept at a region level where there are relatively few values (that is, "east" vs. "west"). What matters may be finer than these—city, ZIP code, even street-level data—but these are harder to aggregate and for human brains to process. We also prefer simple relationships between elements, thinking of relationships as linear because this is easier for us to process. The relationship between price and sales, market penetration and conversion rate, credit risk and income—all are assumed to be linear even when the data suggests otherwise. We even like to conjure up elaborate explanations for trends and variation in data when these are more adequately explained by natural or random variation.

Alas, we are accommodating our biases when we process the data.

Bringing AI into the Workflow

We need to evolve further and bring AI into the workflow as a primary processor of data. For routine decisions that only rely on structured data, we're better off delegating decisions to AI. AI is less prone to human's cognitive bias. (There is a very real risk of using biased data that may cause AI to find specious relationships that are unfair. Be sure to understand how the data is generated in addition to how it is used.) AI can be trained to find segments in the population that best explain variance at fine-grain levels even if they are unintuitive to our human perception. AI has no problem dealing with thousands or even millions of groupings. And AI is more than comfortable working with nonlinear relationships, be they exponential, power laws, geometric series, binomial distributions, or otherwise.

This workflow, which is depicted in figure 12-3, better leverages the information contained in the data and is more consistent and objective in its decisions. It can better determine which ad creative is most effective, the

FIGURE 12-3

A decision-making model that utilizes AI

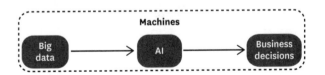

Source: Eric Colson

optimal inventory levels to set, or which financial investments to make.

While humans are removed from this workflow, it's important to note that mere automation is not the goal of an AI-driven workflow. Sure, that may reduce costs, but this is only an incremental benefit. The value of AI lies in making better decisions than what humans alone can do. This creates step-change improvement in efficiency and enables new capabilities.

Leveraging Both AI and Human Processors in the Workflow

Removing humans from workflows that only involve the processing of structured data does not mean that humans are obsolete. There are many business decisions that depend on more than just structured data. Vision statements, company strategies, corporate values, and market dynamics are all examples of information that is only available in our minds and transmitted through culture and other forms of nondigital communication. This information is inaccessible to AI and extremely relevant to business decisions.

For example, AI may objectively determine the right inventory levels to maximize profits. However, in a competitive environment a company may opt for higher inventory levels in order to provide a better customer experience, even at the expense of profits. In other cases, AI may determine that investing more dollars in marketing will have the highest ROI among the options available to the company. However, a company may choose to temper growth in order to uphold quality standards. The additional information available to humans in the form of strategy, values, and market conditions can merit a departure from the objective rationality of AI. In such cases, AI can be used to generate possibilities from which humans can pick the best alternative given the additional information they have access to. The order of execution for such workflows is case-specific. Sometimes AI is first to reduce the workload on humans (see figure 12-4). In other cases, human judgment can provide input for AI processing. In other cases still, there may be iteration between AI and human processing.

The key is that humans are not interfacing directly with data but rather with the possibilities produced by AI's processing of the data. Values, strategy, and culture allow us to reconcile our decisions with objective rationality. This is best done explicitly and fully informed. By leveraging both AI and humans we can make better decisions than by using either one alone.

FIGURE 12-4

A decision-making model that combines the power of AI and human judgment

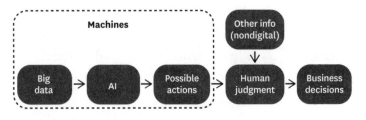

Source: Eric Colson

The Next Phase in Our Evolution

Moving from data-driven to AI-driven is the next phase in our evolution. Embracing AI in our workflows affords better processing of structured data and allows humans to contribute in ways that are complementary.

This evolution is unlikely to occur within the individual organization, just as evolution by natural selection does not take place within individuals. Rather, it's a selection process that operates on a population. The more efficient organizations will survive at a higher rate. Since it's hard for mature companies to adapt to changes in the environment, I suspect we'll see the emergence of new companies that embrace both AI and human contributions from the beginning and build them natively into their workflows.

Many companies have adopted a "data-driven" approach to operational decision making. But humans have limitations when it comes to sorting information and analyzing data. To fully leverage the value of data, companies need to bring in AI.

- ✓ Human decision making is inherently flawed, as we fall victim to heuristics and cognitive biases that affect our judgment.

- ✓ AI can provide the opportunity to sort through vast amounts of data and offer more objective decisions. For routine decisions that rely on structured data, we're better off delegating decisions to AI, as it has no issue sorting through vast amounts of data.

- ✓ Many other business decisions—vision statements, company strategies, etc.—require a mix of AI and human judgment. In these instances, AI should be used to generate the possibilities, from which humans can pick the best alternative.

Adapted from content posted on hbr.org, July 8, 2019 (product #H050C4).

13

HOW COMPANIES CAN USE THE DATA THEY COLLECT TO FURTHER THE PUBLIC GOOD

by Edward L. Glaeser, Hyunjin Kim, and Michael Luca

B y the end of 2017, Yelp had amassed more than 140 million reviews of local businesses. While the company's mission focuses on helping people find local businesses more easily, this wealth of data has the potential to serve other purposes. For instance, Yelp data might help restaurants understand which markets they should consider entering or whether to add a bar. It can help real estate investors understand where gentrification might occur. And it might help private equity firms with an interest in coffee decide whether to invest in Philz or Blue Bottle.

The potential value of the large data sets being amassed by private companies raises new opportunities and challenges for managers making strategic data decisions. While there are plenty of well-publicized examples of data repurposing gone wrong, we think it would be a shame for companies to decide the only option is to hoard their data. Before you decide that your data can't be put to a new use, consider how it might help augment public data sources.

For example, in a recent paper, we explored the potential for Yelp data to measure local economic change and augment the official data, often from the U.S. census, which has long been the bread and butter of economic analyses.[1] Our motivation was simple: Census data is valuable but can be slow-moving and coarse. Public-facing census data can tell you whether more restaurants are opening in a ZIP code, but only after several years. Yelp data can tell you, almost in real time, not only whether restaurants are opening in a ZIP code but even whether more-affordable restaurants are opening on a specific block. We found that Yelp data can help to meaningfully predict trends in the local economy well before census data becomes available, especially in more urban, more educated, and wealthier parts of the country.

This speaks to the broader potential for data from online platforms to improve our understanding of all of America. Just as Yelp can shed light on local economic changes, Zillow could inform our understanding of housing markets, LinkedIn could provide insight about labor markets, and Glassdoor could teach us about the quality of employment options in an area. Companies increasingly recognize the possibility of repurposing their data in these ways for the public good. But repurposing data can have benefits for a company far beyond the warm glow of having done some good. As researchers work with the data, new insights about their data and platform design choices may surface. As policy makers rely on the insights from the data, new relationships can form and facilitate valuable collaborations. Public-facing data efforts can also increase awareness of a company's brand—allowing companies to do well by doing good.

Of course, there are times when repurposing data is not an option, because the data is either sensitive or not that useful. But we often see examples in which a potentially successful use of a new data source fails to deliver because of poor execution.

Drawing on our academic research assessing repurposed data sources, as well as our work with organizations, we see that simple guiding principles can help companies understand how to successfully repurpose their data.

Principle 1: Understand your unique perspective

When deciding whether and how to use your data, it's crucial to take the time to understand whether this information has real value relative to what people already have access to. Start by looking for the best data available. Choose a broadly accepted benchmark, and set a narrow goal to see whether and where you can meaningfully add value.

When looking at Yelp data, for example, we considered census data a significant benchmark, since it is something commonly used in research and policy work. And we set the narrow goal of understanding whether Yelp data can augment existing data points with additional variables and provide more up-to-date information (since it's updated in real time, while the census happens every 10 years). This flavor of incremental improvements can, paradoxically, lead to the largest gains, by making sure that you are going down the right path.

Principle 2: Develop credible analyses

For every exciting new use of digital data that we've come across, we've seen countless others fail to deliver. Successfully repurposing data requires taking benchmarks seriously and cross-validating against them. If your data doesn't match existing benchmarks, then you have to understand why. If the differences are irreconcilable, then you might reconsider the value of your data on that dimension. And if you do go forward with using the data, it's important to think through the best approach to analysis, taking the mismatch into account.

Credible analytics also requires understanding—and being transparent about—the strengths and limitations of your data. Returning to the Yelp example, we highlighted the strengths above. One limitation is that Yelp coverage varies over time and across places. Maintaining credibility and making the most of the data requires understanding and factoring this and other limitations into the analysis and conclusions drawn from the data.

Principle 3: Build partnerships

Even a company that has a great internal data team may not have the right skills to produce public-facing data that will have a real impact. Working with outside researchers and policy makers can help you gauge general interest, build a product that will have credibility, and develop insights that will create value for a broader audience.

There is no such thing as a perfect data set. This is both why new data sources are valuable and why repurposing data can be hard. Tech companies are now collecting unprecedented amounts of data, and they have the potential to greatly improve our understanding of the economy and policy. Yelp ratings are now being used for a variety of purposes, including predicting which restaurants are most likely to have health code violations, identifying which businesses will be impacted by increases to the minimum wage, and shedding light on how gentrifying neighborhoods are evolving.[2] Other platforms have similar potential. And when done carefully and incrementally, each platform adds one piece to the puzzle, leading to a deeper and more nuanced understanding of the economy—all the while harvesting benefits for the company.

TAKEAWAYS

Companies are sitting on troves of data that could benefit society. While there are plenty of examples of data repurposing gone wrong, it would be a shame for companies to decide that the only option is to hoard their data. Simple guiding principles can help companies understand how to repurpose their data successfully.

- ✓ When deciding whether or how to share data for the public good, consider how it might augment information people already have access to. Look for the best data available. Then, choose a broadly accepted benchmark, and set a narrow goal to see whether and where you can meaningfully add value.

- ✓ If your data doesn't match existing benchmarks, aim to understand why. If the differences are irreconcilable, reconsider the value of your data on that dimension. Understand the strengths and limitations of your data—and be transparent about them.

- ✓ Work with outside researchers and policy makers to gauge general interest in your data, build a product that will have credibility, and develop insights that will create value for a broader audience.

NOTES

1. Edward L. Glaeser, Hyunjin Kim, and Michael Luca, "Nowcasting the Local Economy: Using Yelp Data to Measure Economic Activity," Harvard Business School NOM Unit Working Paper No. 18-022, September 2017.

2. Edward L. Glaeser, Andrew Hillis, Scott Duke Kominers, and Michael Luca, "Crowdsourcing City Government: Using Tournaments to Improve Inspection Accuracy," *American Economic Review* 106, no. 5 (May 2016); Dara Lee Luca and Michael Luca, "Survival of the Fittest: The Impact of the Minimum Wage on Firm Exit," Harvard Business School NOM Unit Working Paper No. 17-088, April 2017, rev. August 2018; and Glaeser et al., "Nowcasting the Local Economy."

Adapted from content posted on hbr.org, May 16, 2018 (product #H04BXA).

About the Contributors

SCOTT BERINATO is a senior editor at *Harvard Business Review* and the author of *Good Charts Workbook: Tips, Tools, and Exercises for Making Better Data Visualizations* (Harvard Business Review Press, 2019) and *Good Charts: The HBR Guide to Making Smarter, More Persuasive Data Visualizations* (Harvard Business Review Press, 2016).

NICHOLAS BLOOM is the William Eberle Professor of Economics at Stanford University and a codirector of the Productivity, Innovation and Entrepreneurship program at the National Bureau of Economic Research.

HUGO BOWNE-ANDERSON, PHD, is a data scientist and educator at DataCamp, as well as the host of the podcast *DataFramed*. Follow him on Twitter @hugobowne.

TOBIAS BRANDT is assistant professor of Business Information Management at Erasmus University's Rotterdam School of Management in the Netherlands.

SUSAN CANTRELL is a senior researcher and writer for Accenture.

ERIC COLSON is chief algorithms officer at Stitch Fix. Prior to that he was vice president of Data Science and Engineering at Netflix. Follow him on Twitter @ericcolson.

THOMAS H. DAVENPORT is the President's Distinguished Professor in Management and Information Technology at Babson College, a research fellow at the MIT Initiative on the Digital Economy, and a senior adviser at Deloitte Analytics. He is the author of over a dozen management books, most recently *Only Humans Need Apply: Winners and Losers in the Age of Smart Machines* and *The AI Advantage*.

EDWARD L. GLAESER is the Fred and Eleanor Glimp Professor of Economics at Harvard.

NIKLAS GOBY is a data scientist at ZF, a global automotive supplier based in Friedrichshafen, Germany, and a PhD candidate at the University of Freiburg, also in Germany.

HYUNJIN KIM is a doctoral candidate in the strategy unit at Harvard Business School. Her research explores how organizations can improve strategic decision making and productivity in the digital economy.

CASSIE KOZYRKOV is the chief decision scientist at Google.

CHRIS LITTLEWOOD is the chief innovation and product officer of filtered.com, an edtech company that uses AI to lift productivity by making learning recommendations. Follow him on Twitter @filtered_chris.

MICHAEL LUCA is the Lee J. Styslinger III Associate Professor of Business Administration at Harvard Business School and a coauthor (with Max Bazerman) of *The Power of Experiments: Decision Making in a Data-Driven World*.

DIRK NEUMANN is a professor and chair of Information Systems Research at the University of Freiburg, Germany.

NICOLA PIERRI is a PhD candidate at Stanford University.

THOMAS C. REDMAN, "the Data Doc," is president of Data Quality Solutions. He helps companies and people, including startups, multinationals, executives, and leaders at all levels, chart their courses to data-driven futures. He places special emphasis on quality, analytics, and organizational capabilities.

EVA SAGE-GAVIN leads Accenture's Talent & Organization practice.

ERIC SIEGEL, PHD, is the founder of the Predictive Analytics World and Deep Learning World conference series and executive editor of *The Predictive Analytics Times*. He is the author of the award-winning book *Predictive Analytics: The Power to Predict Who Will Click, Buy, Lie, or Die*, the host of *The Dr. Data Show* web series, a former Columbia University professor, and a renowned speaker, educator, and leader in the field. Follow him on Twitter @predictanalytic.

JOEL SHAPIRO, JD, PHD, is clinical associate professor and executive director of the program on data analytics at Northwestern's Kellogg School of Management.

ELLYN SHOOK is chief leadership and human resources officer for Accenture.

DAVE SUTTON is president and CEO at TopRight, an Atlanta-based strategic marketing firm that serves Global 2000 companies. He's also the author of *Marketing, Interrupted*.

Index

Is Your Business Ready for the Future?

If you enjoyed this book and want more on today's pressing business topics, turn to other books in the **Insights You Need** series from *Harvard Business Review*. Featuring HBR's latest thinking on topics critical to your company's success—from Blockchain and Cybersecurity to AI and Agile—each book will help you explore these trends and how they will impact you and your business in the future.

FOR MORE VISIT HBR.ORG/BOOKS

Engage with HBR content the way you want, on any device.

With HBR's new subscription plans, you can access world-renowned **case studies** from Harvard Business School and receive **four free eBooks**. Download and customize prebuilt **slide decks and graphics** from our **Visual Library**. With HBR's archive, top 50 best-selling articles, and five new articles every day, HBR is more than just a magazine.

Subscribe Today
hbr.org/success